CHRISTIAN DEVIATIONS

CHRISTIAN DEVIATIONS

ESSAYS IN DEFENCE OF THE CHRISTIAN FAITH

HORTON DAVIES

SCM PRESS LTD
56 BLOOMSBURY STREET
LONDON

To

MY FORMER SOUTH AFRICAN
COLLEAGUES AND STUDENTS
IN THE PIONEERING
DEPARTMENT OF DIVINITY
OF RHODES UNIVERSITY
WITH AFFECTIONATE REGARD

First published March 1954
Reprinted May 1954
Reprinted August 1954
Reprinted January 1955
Reprinted February 1956
Reprinted May 1957

Printed in Great Britain by
Northumberland Press Limited
Gateshead on Tyne

CONTENTS

PREFATORY NOTE

ALTHOUGH this brief study in distortions of Christianity is entitled *Christian Deviations*, it does not follow that all the religious communities encountered in these pages are equally far ' from the centre '. The reader may fairly ask the author to define what he means by ' the centre '. By this conception is intended the great historic Communions of Christendom, which accept the Lordship of Jesus Christ as recorded in the Scriptures of the Old and New Testaments and to which the Creeds bear witness. These, with the outstanding exception of the Roman Catholic Church, have associated themselves in the World Council of Churches.

What is offered here is a modest attempt at Christian Apologetics, a defence of the historic Christian faith by distinguishing it from those systems which imitate it and yet distort it by misinterpretation or unwarrantable addition to the essentials of Christian belief. Theosophy, Christian Science, Spiritism, Seventh-Day Adventism, Jehovah's Witnesses and Mormonism, represent in greater or lesser degree the fusion of Christian and non-Christian elements. Their deviations are dangerous distortions of the common and historic Christian faith and their adherents include many former and uninstructed members of the Churches. Sometimes these heretical and schismatical bodies came into being to emphasize facets of the Christian faith and life which had been neglected by the Churches, and on this account their protests may be salutary, in some respects, as reminders of ecclesiastical dereliction of duty.

British-Israel and Moral Re-armament are in a different category. For they represent a theory and a way of spiritual discipline, respectively, which is not deliberately antagonistic to the Christian faith. In fact, many of their members still retain their association with the historic Churches. They fall under censure because the British-Israel theory is a racialistic distortion of our faith and because the Oxford Group is dangerously apathetic to Christian doctrine and the wider fellowship of Christ's Church.

Astrology and Open-air Religion are examples of pagan superstition and credulity, such as might be expected to reappear in an increasingly secularized age.

The relevance of this study is that it offers one way of loving God with all our mind. Christians, it cannot be too emphatically stated, are made, not born. The young men and women who have to fight the good fight of faith intellectually, as well as spiritually, in the universities and colleges, the offices and factories of the modern world, ought to be able to give a reason for their faith and for their preference for the historic Christian faith to its religious alternatives. It is also by the use of reason, 'the candle of the Lord', that the darkness of doubt and difficulty is removed, and the mind is prepared for the active reception of Divine Revelation.

I

A SURVEY OF
CHRISTIANITY'S RIVALS

Jesus said, 'I am the way, the truth, and the life;
no one cometh unto the Father, but by me.'
(John 14.6)

FROM the first day of the Christian Church, Christians have had to fight the battle of faith on two fronts: spiritual and intellectual. While the martyrs outlived and outdied their opponents, the apologists out-thought them.

The task of apologetics, the intellectual defence of the Christian faith, changes from age to age, as new opponents arise to challenge Christian doctrine. None the less, throughout Church history the systems that rival Christianity appear to fall into four main classes: (1) the denial of spiritual values and of the existence of God, which may be termed atheism on its intellectual side, and materialism or secularism on its cultural and social side; (2) the claims to finality made by religions other than Christianity; (3) a Judaistic perversion of the Christian faith; (4) a Gnostic eclecticism, and anthology of Christian and non-Christian beliefs. Our concern is exclusively with the perversions and distortions of Christianity such as are included within the third and fourth categories.

I

The first council of the Christian Church in Jerusalem had to face the living issue: how much Judaism shall non-Jewish converts to the Christian faith be expected to embrace? Was the Law valid now that Christians lived under the sphere of grace? Judaistic Christianity has sometimes been described as the retention of the scaffolding even when the headstone of the corner has been placed in position: that is, an attempt to gain salvation by obedience to the prescriptions of the Jewish Law, instead of a life of trust in the merits and mediation of Jesus Christ in the strength of the Holy Spirit. Many Christians in all centuries have found it difficult to accept the ethical imperative of love. They would prefer to regard their religion as the observance of a code of prohibitions, rather than believe, with St. Augustine of Hippo, that the Christian has only one relevant injunction, ' love God and do what you like '. The ethic of the second-mile is both more exacting and more exhilarating, and it does not appeal to cautious souls. Thus, from the earliest days, legalism has always fought against the life of the Spirit. The other persistently-recurring element of Judaism within Christianity has been millenarianism, and, moreover, one more material than spiritual in its allocation of rewards to the faithful.

The Judaistic heresies within cults claiming to be Christian are: Seventh-Day Adventism, Jehovah's Witnesses, British-Israel and Mormonism. Seventh-Day Adventism revives sabbatarianism, making it a doctrine essential for salvation, and in its millenarianism limits the number of the elect to its own members. The Jehovah's Witnesses develop their doctrine of soul-sleep and their millenarianism on an Old Testament foundation. They, too, circumscribe salvation by limiting it to their own communion. The British-Israelites have reduced the doctrine of election to favouritism and their God to an Anglo-Saxon tribal deity. The patriarchal ethics and the apocalypticism of Mormonism reflects a Judaistic, rather than a Christian, colouring. The success of these Judaistic perversions of Christianity forces on Christians the question: What home truths have these sects to teach the Churches? These lessons appear to be three. Firstly, their adherents have a knowledge of the contents of the Holy Scriptures which Christians would do well to emulate. The Bible is the record of the revelation of the mighty acts of God consummated in the life, death, resurrection and ascension of Jesus Christ, and the donation of the Holy Spirit; it is the supreme witness to the origin of our faith, and trust in Christ as the contemporary Lord is re-created and nourished by it. For this reason alone it is imperative that Christians should become again the people of the Book. The very facility with which adherents of Judaistic sects cite chapter and verse of the Scriptures and the enthusiasm with which Communists con their 'Red Bible', *Das Kapital* of Karl Marx, should drive Christians back to the Word as their iron-rations and marching orders.

But that is not enough, for clearly a thorough knowledge of the Bible has not prevented the sectarians from becoming heretics. In the second place, what is required is a *critical* knowledge of the Holy Writ. Biblicism becomes heretical because it has no standard of reference by which to evaluate the different parts of the Scriptures. Claiming to believe that the Bible is equally inspired in all its parts, it nevertheless builds on private interpretation of a selection of the Law and of the Apocalyptic parts of Scripture. The only adequate criterion is 'the mind of Christ' by which Christians understand the life of our Lord as recorded in those superb biographies, the Gospels, and in the leading of the Holy Spirit given to the Apostles and recorded in the other books of the New Testament. This standard disenthralls the Christian from the authority of the Old Dispensation and translates him 'into the kingdom of the love of God's dear Son'. For 'the Law came by Moses, but grace and truth by Christ'. His ethical motivation is the constraint of the love of Christ. The morality of justice under the Old Dispensation is replaced by the profounder understanding of forgiveness which is, according to Dr. Reinhold Niebuhr, 'the crown of Christian ethics'. Whatever in the Old Covenant is contrary to the attitude or the acts of Christ is un-Christian or sub-Christian, and therefore of no authority for the Christian man. In particular, a critical understanding of the Scriptures liberates the Christian

from regarding prophetical and apocalyptic books as crypto-
grams from which the ingenious Bibliolater may predict the
future in detail.[1]

The success of these heretical cults should, in fact, force the
Christian Church to attempt a thorough revaluation not only
of the Bible, but of the Holy Spirit and of the Church itself
as the source of authority for Christian doctrine. History has
shown that the Bible of itself, when regarded as infallible and
equally inspired in all its parts, leads to the formation of
heretical sects. It also shows that an exclusive dependence
upon the Holy Spirit leads to such aberrations as characterized
the fantastic ' rule of the saints ' in the days of the Commonwealth in England, when every man claimed his idiosyncrasies
as new revelations; and that exclusive dependence upon the
Church as the organ of truth leads to the propounding of
unbiblical doctrines, such as the Assumption of the Blessed
Virgin and the Immaculate Conception, as of the essence of
the faith. The Bible, the Church, and the individual inspired
by the Holy Spirit are three interlocking authorities for the
Christian faith. It is also possible that the Bible is of primary,
the Church of secondary, and the inspired individual of ter-
tiary importance, but this problem has still to be solved. The
heretics may be thanked for this at least, that they are forcing
the contemporary Church to realize its urgency.

In the third place, the ' Judaistic ' heretics have an enthusiasm in communicating their erratic tenets which Christians
would do well to emulate in the spreading of the truth as it is
in Christ Jesus. As instances of this we may take the remarkable organization of the Jehovah's Witnesses which obliges
each of their members to canvass every householder in the
interests of their doctrines, so much so that they have become
a by-word for importunity and pertinacity, and the missionary
zeal of the Seventh-Day Adventists and Mormons who have
a reputation second only to the Moravians for the high proportion of their adherents who become missionaries in all parts

[1] *Vide* H. Cunliffe-Jones, *The Authority of the Biblical Revelation*. (Jas.
Clarke).

of the earth. The warning of Professor J. R. Coates is timely:

' The success of heresies and unorthodox cults is a measure
of the failure of the Church. As with Spiritualism, Christian
Science, and Adventism, so with British-Israel: its propa-
gandists minister to real human needs, and its plausibility
is largely due to its ingenuity in relating the Bible to
contemporary experience and to current affairs.'[2]

II

Several other cults brought under review belong to the
Gnostic type of heresy. They represent attempts to combine
elements of Christian teaching with doctrines of other systems
or faiths. The early Christians had to counter not only a
Judaising tendency but also a Hellenistic movement. Dr. Radford rightly explains the attractions of such eclecticism as due

' partly to the desire to combine non-Christian ideas with
Christian ideas, or to winning outsiders by going as near
as possible to their position, and in still larger part to the
wish of thinking men to understand and explain the
Christian faith for thinking men '.[3]

Many philosophers have attempted to find a common religion
which summed up the spiritual values of all religions from
the days of Lord Herbert of Cherbury to our contemporary,
Professor Hocking of Harvard. To them doctrine was the
ineffectual attempt of the different religions to capture in
words the ineffable experiences of the mystics and the
moralists. They argued that it ought to be possible to express
the same experiences in common concepts. The renewed
impetus to provide a common religion for humanity derives
partly from the comparative study of religion, partly from the

---

[2] *Expository Times,* Vol. LIV, p. 313.
[3] *Ancient Heresies in Modern Dress* (Robertson, Melbourne, 1913), p. 34.

conviction that it is better for an increasingly secular civilization to have one religion rather than none, and partly from a desire to end nationalism and internecine warfare by acknowledging an overarching loyalty to one authoritative creed. Whilst several religions have been considered for the honour of being acclaimed the universal religion of mankind, the Christian faith has been found wanting by philosophers both because of its claim for finality and for its 'scandal of particularity'. Christians have stubbornly refused to allow their Saviour to consort on terms of equality in their estimation with Confucius, the Buddha, or Mohammed, the 'seal of the prophets'. Thus their claim that the Incarnation of the eternal Son of God is the final revelation of the nature and activity of God makes them unable to relegate the Christ to a convenient Pantheon in which all religious teachers are worshipped alike. The anchor of their faith in history, as recorded in the saga of the mighty acts of God, means that Christianity cannot be reduced to a philosophy.

Examples of the Gnostic type of heresy are Theosophy, Spiritism, and Christian Science. Its adherents are often former Christians. Of contemporary Gnosticism, Dr. Radford says:

' The creed by which the Christian Scientist explains the facts of faith-healing is a latter-day Gnosticism which denies not merely the spiritual possibilities of the material world but also its reality as an object of experience. Theosophy is a latter-day Gnosticism which dissolves the Gospel into an allegory, fills the spiritual world with the creations of Hindu fancy, and now is summoning Christendom and all other religions to look to the East for another re-incarnation of the Christ-spirit as the world teacher who is to inaugurate a new world-faith.'[4]

We may note that Gnostic eclecticisms have the following features in common. Their religion appeals to the proud

[4] *Ancient Heresies in Modern Dress* (Robertson, Melbourne, 1913), p. 34.

rather than the humble in heart, for it claims to sum up the best in other religions and thus castigates adherents of the older faiths as old-fashioned. Its appeal is largely to intellectuals and initiates and not to the great under-privileged multitudes of the world. Their philosophy is almost always pantheistic and shares the characteristic weaknesses of that outlook; for example, it despises the body which for the Christian is the temple of the Holy Spirit; it teaches an automatic immortality which makes an end of a moral interpretation of history; it depersonalizes God so that He becomes an ' essence ' or a ' principle ' and ceases to be *the* Person; consequently it despises history and the world as illusory, and shows an ostrich-like optimism towards sin, and an unwillingness to change the social conditions, which militate against the full development of personality. Salvation is through identification with God by means of meditation, not by the transformation of the will.

The condemnation of any attempt to find a common religion such as Theosophy is that no religion can be successful which builds only upon the highest common factors in all religions. The history of eighteenth-century Deism in England, with its attempt to banish distinctive doctrines in the interests of a religion that could be accepted by all men of good sense, proves that the resulting creed was ineffectual in the attempt to transform the lives of men. John Howe rightly parodied it as affirming, ' There shall be a God, provided he be not meddlesome '. Furthermore, the different religions do not mix, because they teach different, not common, tenets. Christianity is both world-affirming and world-denying. Buddhism is entirely world-denying. Christianity affirms that God the Father is Creator and Controller of the universe. Buddhism denies the existence of a personal God at all. Yet it is precisely these two religions which Theosophy has tried to combine.

The mistake of Spiritism and Christian Science, which have closer affinities with the Christian Faith, is to attempt to make one Christian tenet into the whole of Christianity. Although

Professor Bethune-Baker was writing of early heresiarchs, his explanation of the motivation of heresy is applicable to both Spiritism and Christian Science. He declares that heterodoxy arose:

> ' when they seized on a few facts as though they were all the facts, and from these few framed theories to explain and interpret all; when they put forward a meagre and immature conception as a full-grown representation of the Christian idea of life '.[5]

In each case the success of these two cults has been due to the failure of the Church to keep in the forefront of its teaching the truths which they seceded to maintain. The Spiritists have reaffirmed the centrality of the doctrine of the Resurrection in the Christian faith, and have taken the belief in the Communion of Saints as the centre and sum of their faith. The Christian Scientists have seen the overwhelming importance of faith in the New Testament narratives and applied it to the sicknesses of humanity. In fact, both the doctrine of the Communion of Saints and the practice of faith-healing are important constituents of the Christian faith and life. These needed to be reaffirmed, but the mistake of the heretics was to assert that these comprehended the entire faith.

It has been already remarked that Gnostic heresies find the readiest converts amongst weak Christians. This provides an obvious lesson for the historic Churches. Their candidates for confirmation or membership must be instructed in the Biblical faith as summarized in the Apostles' Creed, in Christian conduct as summarized in the Decalogue and the Beatitudes, and in Christian devotions as summarized in the Lord's Prayer. A thorough understanding of these is a minimal necessity for every Christian.

A further curious factor in modern heresies which deserves the attention of the Churches is the important part played by women in their foundation and continuance. It is surely

[5] *An Introduction to the Early History of Christian Doctrine*, pp 4-5.

significant that the two founders of Theosophy were Madame Blavatsky and Mrs. Annie Besant, that Christian Science owes its origin to Mrs. Mary Baker Eddy, and that the originator of Seventh-Day Adventism was Mrs. Ellen White. It might be suggested that in each case men had pioneered the thought-forms of the new systems, but none the less the success of these cults is due to the drive of energetic women. Can this fact have any significance for the Churches? One reason for the interest of women in these new faiths is that their place is recognized in their hierarchies, as it is not in the historic Christian Churches. Although Christians have affirmed for almost twenty centuries with St. Paul that 'there is neither male nor female, but all are one in Christ Jesus', this belief does not result in the ordination of women, far less in their elevation to a high place in the government of the Christian Church. Among Roman Catholics there are no female priests, although religious communities of women are encouraged and respected. The same is true of the Orthodox and Anglican Churches, though the Anglican Church regards the order of Deaconesses as 'an apostolic order of the ministry in the Church of God'. Lutherans never and Presbyterians rarely ordain women to any rank of the sacred ministry. Methodists have an Order of Deaconesses, but these are not on a parity with the ministry. Only the Baptists and the Congregationalists have encouraged women to seek ordination, and have given them the same rights and status as male ministers of the Gospel. The Society of Friends does not ordain either men or women, but both sexes have equal rights and privileges. If all the Churches were to remove this form of sexual discrimi-nation, the temptation for devout women to set up their own forms of cult, or to gravitate towards those sects that accord women a higher status, would be greatly reduced. Further-more, it seems that the heretical cults founded by women show a warmth of fellowship that is so often unwarrantably absent in the historic Churches. The same factor may also account for the remarkable success of the Oxford Group Movement.

III

Is it possible to catalogue the tendencies of the sects in such a way as to underline their strength and weakness? The attempt will be made to summarize those factors which two or three of them hold in common, so that Christians may be on their guard against features of the religious life which tend, when unrestrained, to develop into heresies and schisms.

Firstly, there is the danger of mistaking the part for the whole in Christian faith or practice. Two examples are Christian Science and Theosophy.

Secondly, there is the danger of an over-emphasis on the Old Testament to the detriment of the New. Examples of this tendency are Jehovah's Witnesses, Seventh-Day Adventism, Christadelphianism, Mormonism, and British-Israel.

Thirdly, there is the danger of confusing Christianity with Pantheism. Both Theosophy and Christian Science are examples of this confusion.

Fourthly, there is the danger of seeking for greater assurance in the religious life than faith in Christ offers. Spiritism, with its attempt to obtain experimental proof of life after death, is one example, and the predictions of the Millenarian sects provide another. Each is a product of scepticism rather than of trust. The same may also be said of Astrology.

Fifthly, there is the danger of spiritual pride which issues in the schism of a 'holier-than-thou' attitude, or in the formation of an esoteric cult for initiates or intellectuals only. Diverse examples of this characteristic are found in the Oxford Group, Theosophy, and some of the Millenarian sects. The corrective is the charity of the One Holy Catholic and Apostolic Church, of which the historic Communions are branches, honouring individuals of all races and classes and types.

Sixthly, there is the danger of using God as a means to an end. This is the case when God is a convenience for obtaining excellent health in Christian Science, or as a means of obtaining political leadership of the world as in British-Israel.

Seventhly, there is the danger of individualistic pietism, quietism, and a concentration on ' glory for me '. Its correlative is the renunciation of all civic and political responsibilities, and is evinced by Theosophists, Jehovah's Witnesses, Christian Scientists and Seventh-Day Adventists. It also contributed to the success of Marxism by causing the latter to condemn Christianity as ' dope '.

Eighthly, there is the supreme danger of failing to acknowledge the fullness, the uniqueness and the finality of the Christian doctrine of the Incarnation. All the sects suffer from this defect, otherwise they would not have come into being. Where Jesus is thought of as a first-century teacher and inspired prophet, as was often the case in Communions which accepted what was known as a ' reduced Christology ', the way was already open for the displacement of Jesus by later and self-appointed prophets like Ellen White, Mary Baker Eddy, Joseph Smith or Annie Besant. Where He is accepted as the Eternal and only-begotten Son of God, and worshipped as the Lord of lords and King of kings, and obeyed as Master, Christian humility makes it impossible for a mere human to pretend to a better insight into the mind of God than Jesus had.

IV

Finally, Christianity will be victorious over all its rivals when it is most true to its own inheritance. If it cares for the bodies, the souls, and the organization of a just order of society, it will have nothing to fear from Communism. If the fellowship of Christians is a genuine community and family springing from their communion with the God and Father of us all, if Christian members confess their sins in sincerity and with a desire to make reparation to those whom they have wronged, and if they provide a way of life with opportunities of thrilling service for its younger members, Christianity need have nothing to fear from the Oxford Group Movement or Open-air Religion. If it places the doctrines of the resurrection and of the Communion of Saints in the centre of its worship, the spurious attractions of Spiritism will be unavailing because dispelled by faith in the Risen Christ. If Christianity takes seriously the miraculous powers of faith in a wonder-working God, Christian Science will lose its hold on its followers. If Christians really believe that their Lord has won a triple victory over sin, suffering and death, and that ' all things work together for good to them that love God ', they will not relapse into the superstition of Astrology. If the Churches proclaim of Christ by life and by lip that ' there is none other Name whereby we must be saved', Theosophy and indeed all other religions will lose their attractions. If the Church by its abounding charity manifests in its international and interracial fellowship that there is neither ' Jew nor Greek, bond nor free ', and that God is no respecter of persons, all racialistic distortions of the faith such as British-Israel and the German-Christian Movement will earn the unceasing antagonism of Christians. If Christians accept the general promises of Christ, and do not try to implement His reverent silences with details drawn from their own materialistic imaginations, and show a comparable zeal for transmitting their holy faith, then the unscriptural predictions of the Seventh-Day Adventists and Jehovah's Witnesses will deceive no Christian.

In brief, the best defence of the Christian faith is to know and to obey the ' mind of Christ ', who is alone the Way, the Truth and the Life.

II

THEOSOPHY

Beware of anyone getting hold of you by means of a theosophy which is specious make-believe, on the lines of human tradition, corresponding to the elemental spirits of the world and not to Christ.

(Col. 2.8)

PART of the attraction of Theosophy is to be found in its pontifical title. Originally the name meant no more than 'a knowledge of things Divine', a designation which each other religion might claim for its own. In time, however, it came to carry overtones of meaning, implying that this was a superior and unusually intimate knowledge of God, reserved only for the intellectually and spiritually advanced. It further suggested that this esoteric system of doctrines and rites was occult and reserved only for the initiated. Its first appeal, therefore, is clearly to the pride of the elect; in short, to spiritual snobbery.

The other attractions of Theosophy are, it seems, to defend the justice of the moral order, to offer a prospect of spiritual progress here and hereafter, and its profession to deliver its devotees from all constricting theological or ecclesiastical loyalties.

Although it originates from the time of the mystery religions and the Gnostics, its contemporary form has a modern derivation. It commenced when the Theosophical Society was founded by Madame Blavatsky and Colonel Olcott in New York in 1875. The Society was intended to compare the methods of Spiritualism with those of the old Jewish and

Egyptian Cabbalas. America proving too pragmatic and deficient in the appreciation of mysticism, Madame Blavatsky went to India in 1878 where she gained an immediate and widespread success. She gathered a group of enthusiastic Indian and European disciples around her and together they studied the speculations of the Eastern mystics. She claimed to be in touch with the Great White Brotherhood of Tibet who were, in her own words, a 'Lodge of Masters or Adepts' in the spiritual life. The Society for Psychical Research investigated this claim but pronounced it fraudulent. After this exposure in 1885, she left Madras. In the ensuing six years of her life, she produced her book, *Secret Doctrine*, which is the catechism of modern Theosophy. This body of teaching was later systematized and developed by Mrs. Annie Besant, who gained a respectful hearing for Theosophy among intelligent and cultured people. G. K. Chesterton's recipe for Theosophy aptly summarizes its origin: 'Asia, and Evolution and the English lady; and I think they would be better apart.'

It is important to notice that the cult originated in India. The Easterner and the Westerner look through the world with different eyes. The man of the East is naturally a mystic: he is more interested in the inner world of meditation than in the outward world of phenomena and investigation. His religion is apt to be an escape from the world to God. Indeed, he claims to find God by premature retirement from the world.

By contrast, the religion of the man of the West is more a desire to remould the world according to the Divine plan. Edward Vernon declares that the symbol of the East is the temple, while the symbol of the West is the scientific laboratory. The East looks inward, the West outward. Or, in psychological terms, the man of the East is an introvert, while the man of the West is an extrovert. Perhaps, however, the best distinction drawn between East and West in religion is Chesterton's. 'The Buddhist saint,' he said, 'has his eyes shut, whilst the Christian saint has his eyes open.' Theosophy, although it claims to be the universal religion, is very much the product of the East, living in the atmosphere of introspection, asceticism and withdrawal from the world, which characterizes the religions of the East.

I

The claims of Theosophy must now be considered. As previously indicated, its chief claim is to be the universal religion. Had it not borrowed its doctrines almost exclusively from the East, the claim might have some truth in it. In fact, however, the idea of the unknowability of God derives from the Hindu *Upanishads*, the ideal of detachment from an illusory world is borrowed from Buddhism, as also the doctrine of successive human re-incarnations. Furthermore, its methods of attaining to religious peace are all of Eastern origin.

Its claim to be the universal religion cannot be accepted for two other reasons. One is that a religion for spiritual experts only is bound to appeal to a minority, never to the majority, as a universal religion must do. But the most compelling reason against the belief that it is the universal religion is that syncretism takes place only at the cost of destroying all that is distinctive in differing religions. Christianity and Buddhism, for example, will not mix. The Christian ideal of the future life is the perfection of the self, the Buddhist the annihilation of all selfhood.

The second major claim of Theosophy is to be a compound of modern science and ancient philosophy. This is rapidly disposed of by Dr. James Black, as he argues that

'The Eastern speculation of re-incarnation, i.e. souls after death being reborn into another human life, is totally against the proved findings of the science of heredity, where offspring are known to inherit not only their physical life, but also their powers and capabilities from their parents and ancestry.'[1]

[1] *New Forms of the Old Faith* (Nelson, 1948), p. 58.

II

The doctrines of Theosophy can be viewed from three vantage-points.

Their teaching about God. Theosophists are Pantheists. In their own words: ' All that is is God, and God is all that is.' This insistence upon the unity of God seems to be admirable, until it is examined. When pushed to its logical conclusion, however, its absurdity is patent. If God is everything and everything is God, then God is as much in an archangel as in an atom-bomb, as much in the sunset as in the seaweed, as much in a cherub as in a crocodile, as much in ameliorative medicine as in a microbe, and as much in a martyr as in a mosquito.

But, the Theosophist hastens to explain, all these things were created by God and God wills them to exist. It is true that they are the materials for our human struggle, the fulcrum for our spiritual leverage; but it is idle to pretend that God is indifferent as to whether the microbe slays the man, or the man slays the microbe. Then the Theosophist replies scathingly, ' But you are mistaken. It is foolish to describe God as personal. Would you endow God with the limitations of a finite human personality? He is neither interested nor disinterested, because God is not a He at all. He is suprapersonal.'

It is here that the argument breaks off, because the term ' God' is interpreted differently by the Christian and the Theosophist. What the Christian regards as the noblest way of defining God, the Theosophist takes as an insult to his Deity. If both Christian and Theosophist regard the world as a prison-house, there the agreement ends. The Theosophist is eagerly searching for a key with which to escape. The Christian, on the other hand, is thinking of the other poor spirits confined in the same prison. He is eager to transform convicts into reformed characters. The Christian's greatest stimulus to reformation is the belief that Christ demands that he love his neighbour as himself. He is the brother for whom Christ died. For the Christian, therefore, the world is neither good nor bad; it is neutral. It is the school of character, 'the vale of soul-making', the edge which sharpens the soul into an instrument to improve the world. The Theosophist says, 'I accept', or 'I resign'. The Christian says, 'I resist'.

The fundamental difference in outlook is due to a basic difference in the conception of God. The Theosophist's God is impersonal Justice. The Christian's God co-operates with man to make all things work together for good.

In addition, Theosophy falls under censure for its inherent contradiction. For, while it urges that God is impersonal, the 'Super-consciousness', the Deity is given such personal attributes as 'loving', 'just', and 'truthful'.

Furthermore, the Christology of the Theosophists is seriously defective and arbitrarily unhistorical. Mrs. Besant has had the effrontery to produce her own Gospel. According to her, Jesus was born a hundred years before His presumed nativity, was trained in a desert community of the Essenes, where He learned the esoteric wisdom of the East from visiting Indian and Egyptian sages. She further maintains that the 'Christ' part of His nature was added at Baptism but withdrawn during the Crucifixion and that He returned to teach His disciples the mysteries for a period of fifty years. She equates Jesus with Buddha and Confucius as one of the Masters of the spiritual life. Christian orthodoxy cannot accept this caricature of the Founder of the Faith.

The Theosophist teaching about man and salvation. The Theosophists have a peculiar doctrine of man. They assert that each individual is compounded of seven parts. The most common classification is the following: the physical body, the etheric double (or vital body), the astral (or emotional) body, the mental body, the causal body, the future body, the perfected body. Salvation consists in moving from body to body until perfection is reached in the seventh body. Successively, the unimportant parts of the self are sloughed off like the unwanted skins of a snake. Or, in the biting words of Father Bede Frost, this is ' the strip-tease of the soul '.

What is to be thought of this teaching concerning the seven parts or bodies of man? To say the least of it, it is very muddled psychology. Man cannot be divided into physical, vital, emotional, mental and volitional parts and retain the unity of his personality. All these faculties of man are employed simultaneously, not successively. A simple instance may be taken—that of a footballer scoring a goal. The kick is physical, the placing of the kick is mental, the fact that the toe connects with the ball is vital, the will to kick is volitional, and the joy that a good kick brings is emotional; these are all parts of one simultaneous reaction and action. They are only divisible on reflection, not in action. Indeed, if they took place successively, it is doubtful if any footballer would ever score a goal! Human personality cannot be divided into five parts, let alone seven. As for the future body or the perfect body, there seems to be no relation between them and the present personality of man. This psychology is confused because it isolates parts of human life that co-exist and refuse to be parted in the actual texture of experience.

But an even more serious criticism must be offered of the salvation envisaged by the Theosophists. It consists in killing the body that the soul may live. But the body is not evil, it is the instrument of the soul. It is the medium through which the soul communicates with the outer world and with other souls. What alone is evil is the abuse of the body.

Theosophists make the mistake of saying, ' Get rid of the body and you get rid of evil '. But, as Jesus reminded His disciples, it is evil thoughts that corrupt, not the body. Salvation must be wrought in the inner citadel of the mind and imagination; therefore there is no real salvation to be found in mortifying the body, which is only the agent of evil thoughts and imaginings. Evil is not like a stain on the polished table that soils the surface; it is far more akin to dry rot that weakens and then destroys the interior of the wood. Humanity needs a new inner constitution, but the Theosophists offer us only French polishing. Our need is not evolution, but revolution.

The teaching about re-incarnation. This is the most distinctive and important Theosophical tenet. It is this aspect of Theosophy which has attracted several men of distinction in the Western world, including Aldous Huxley and J. B. Priestley. In fact, the fine series of 'Time-plays' written by Priestley have this as their central theme.

Like Christians, Theosophists have to unravel the age-old problem of the suffering of the innocent. How can they reconcile this with the belief in a wise and benevolent God? The Christian admits the difficulty. His tentative answer is that since we are bound together as families and nations the innocent must suffer with the guilty for that is the price to be paid for human fellowship. Moreover, since God suffers in the afflictions of His people this tragic experience can be transmuted to gain where it is accepted in faith, for suffering then becomes an impetus to Christian love.

Theosophy takes an easier path. It denies that there is any problem, since it denies that there are any innocent persons. We are all supposed to be suffering for sins committed in previous existences or reaping the advantages of previous virtues. We therefore deserve the penalties or rewards dealt out to us in this life. Thus if we are born diseased or defective, or in the midst of crime or poverty, it is the recompense of our former evil deeds; if we have noble dispositions, great abilities, or high positions, these were won by our own former merits. This is undeniably an attractive belief because it reconciles the suffering in the world with the justice of God.

Its fundamental weakness lies in its failure to explain how suffering does benefit us. If I was a murderer in my last life and I am born deformed in this life, it is a judgment that I deserve. But, since I cannot recall the circumstances under which I was prompted to commit murder, how can such a judgment teach me repentance? How can I repent sins whose origin and nature I have forgotten? Since I cannot feel sorry, how can I improve? Moreover, if I am born deformed, I have no information to assure me that it was a just punishment. Is there more reason why I should say, ' I deserve it ', than that I should curse the universe for my misfortune? These are some of the obstinate questions the doctrine of re-incarnation provokes in Christian minds.

Furthermore, Theosophy, while professing to explain the inequalities of life, succeeds only in making them disappear in the mists of the past. We are then forced to ask, What caused the first unequal conditions or the first unequal actions?

Possibly the worst feature of the doctrine of re-incarnation is that it paralyses the desire to improve the social environment and produces an ignoble fatalism. Since action is the fruit of desire, and desire must be abandoned, action is prohibited.

Moreover, it is no palliation to be told that things will be better in another existence. We wish to make the best of this life here and now. This belief in an impersonal justice has no dynamic in it. It is a conservatism of the soul, a religion of long-deferred hope.

Even the future life posited by Theosophy is only a pale shadow of the Christian doctrine of eternal life, not only because its realization may be almost indefinitely postponed, but also because it offers absorption or annihilation of individuality in the Infinite as its goal. The Christian doctrine of the perfection of the self is its complete contrary.

III

The chief criticism of Theosophy is that it appeals to the self-regarding motives. Its advice is, ' Make it easier for yourself in the next life '. This plea must be rejected by the Christian because he is not concerned primarily for a more comfortable existence in another world for himself; he wants a finer existence for his brethren in this world. He desires to be a reformer, not a pensioner. He cannot worship a God who is impartial justice. How can the thought of a Divine pair of scales either inspire or comfort him? He needs a God who bleeds with humanity in its wounds and scars. He wants a God who will redeem society and remake man in His own image. He requires a saviour and a friend. He therefore turns to God's eternal and beloved Son, the carpenter of Nazareth, whose hands are blunted in life's workshop, the loving Teacher and Companion of the common people. He turns to the lonely crucified Son of God on the stark hill-top, who took His station among thieves.

The God of the Theosophists is too highbrow for the Christian. Their God is no more interested in our human struggle than a sleeping and gigantic elephant. The God of the Theosophists is busied with his mathematical calculations, apportioning exact retribution to our sins in different existences. His Impersonal Highness is, in short, merely a celestial calculating-machine.

Christians cannot be persuaded to leave the God who met them in Christ Jesus and, without any assurance save their need, embraced them in the arms outspread on the jagged tree of Calvary. They stake their life on the fact that this God cares, because He treats our erring humanity so patiently; because, also, ' He gave His only-begotten Son that whosoever believeth on Him should not perish but have everlasting life '. Christ is the proof that God cares. In Him God gave us His Word.

IV

The grandeur of the Christian faith is seen in comparison with the deficiencies in Theosophy which it can supply. Christianity offers us a true view of sin. For the Theosophist a sense of personal sin is thought of as weak and degrading. Forgiveness, too, is inadmissible for the Theosophist because it would represent a diminution of strict justice. No new start is possible for the Theosophist in this life, but only in the next, and a man must work out his own slow salvation without the assistance of God.

There is no redemption from the power of evil in Theosophy, either. The World Teachers or Bodhisattvas of Theosophy offer teaching and enlightenment and, occasionally, example. But human nature needs more—it requires the infusion of new life. It is only Jesus Christ who said, ' I am come that they might have life and have it more abundantly '.

Theosophy knows nothing of the meaning of sacrifice, which includes vicarious suffering. Their ideal man practises detachment to kill desire. But this is a striking contrast to the Saviour, who ' though He was a Son, yet learned obedience through the things which He suffered ', who ' was in all points tempted like as we are, yet without sin ', who, as the Sinless Penitent, ' hath borne our griefs and carried our sorrows '.

Because of Christ's coming to serve the world, Christians cannot be content with their own salvation. They can rest only when the kingdoms of this world have become kingdoms of our God and of His Christ. There is only one faith to live by: the faith of the Apostles, enshrined in the Creed of that name. This has been admirably summed up by Dr. Norman Macleod thus: ' There is a Father in Heaven who loves us, a Brother who died for us, and a Spirit who helps us to be good, and a Home where we shall all meet at the last.' That is a creed that will see humanity through this life into the next. It is, if need be, a creed to die for; it is assuredly a creed to live for.

III

CHRISTIAN SCIENCE

*Who in the days of his flesh, having offered up
prayers and supplications with strong crying and
tears . . . though he was a Son, yet learned
obedience by the things which he suffered.*

(Heb. 5.7-8)

CHRISTIAN SCIENCE is the most recent and, in Protestant
countries, the most effective religious rival of the historic
Christian faith. It bears so manifestly the hall-mark of its
founder, Mary Baker Eddy, that it is impossible to understand
it apart from the spiritual odyssey of that lady.

She was born in 1821 in the New Hampshire town of Bow,
being the sixth child of a gentleman-farmer and his wife,
who were respected members of the Congregational Church.
She was a highly sensitive child who reacted strongly against
the stern and forbidding Calvinism of her father's creed. Her
later teaching was formulated in antagonism to the unchal-
lenged Calvinist tenet that trials and sorrows are natural and
inevitable and are sent by God for the spiritual strengthening
of His children. During most of her childhood she was subject to a serious nervous illness which continued through many
years of adulthood. She was not only unfortunate in having
an unsympathetic father, but also an unsympathetic husband.
Her first husband was a building-contractor, whose profits
were made by the exploitation of the slaves he owned. Soon
after the marriage, he died of yellow fever, leaving her with
a small son and considerable assets. These she employed in
freeing the slaves and in educating her child. The young

widow then married a dentist. So physically enfeebled was the bride that Dr. Patterson had to carry her downstairs from her room for the ceremony and return her there on its completion. Patterson was also a scapegrace, who became infatuated with other women and left her to bring up her ailing child alone. However, he performed one good turn for his wife by introducing her to an unorthodox healer, renowned throughout New England as Phineas P. Quimby. He was a man of great personal magnetism. It was he who gave her the hints upon which she was to build up her system of Christian Science. He claimed that there was only one cure for all diseases—the confidence of the patient in the healer.

He described his healing art in the following fashion: 'My practice,' he said, 'is unlike all medical practice. I give no medicine, and make no outward applications. I tell the patient his troubles, and what he thinks is his disease, and my explanation is the cure. If I succeed in correcting his errors, I change the fluids of the system, and establish the patient in health. The truth is the cure.'

Mrs. Eddy's indebtedness to Quimby was greater than she cared to admit. His manuscripts, which have since been published, reveal that he referred to his new mind-healing system as 'Christian Science', and that he called disease 'an error', and this is, in fact, the most distinctive doctrine associated with the name of Mary Baker Eddy. 'Disease,' he wrote, 'is false reasoning. False reasoning is sickness and death.' On his death in 1866, Mrs. Eddy did not merely repudiate her indebtedness to Quimby, but went so far as to claim that he had borrowed these ideas from her. Her conceited desire to claim absolute originality for her teaching resulted in the palpable untruth she wrote in her compendium of Christian Science:

'No human pen nor tongue taught me the science contained in the book.'[1]

Mary Baker Patterson (as she was then named), presented

[1] *Science and Health* (Bird), p. 110.

herself in October 1862 at the International Hotel, Portland, Maine, to this Phineas P. Quimby. He told her that her animal spirit was reflecting its grief upon her body, and calling it spinal disease. He then dipped his hands in water, rubbed her head violently, and sent her into a mesmeric sleep. She awoke cured of her pain. The next day he repeated the treatment; the cure was as complete as it was swift. Moreover, there was no relapse. Her disease, she explained to Quimby, was cured by the healer's understanding of the truth of Christ brought by Him into the world and lost for centuries, and not by Quimby's mesmerism. Quimby denied this, being an arrant unbeliever. But his patient refused to accept his disclaimer, and was so far restored to health that she mounted the hundred and eighty-two steps to the Dome of the City Hall to advertise to the world the greatness of Quimby.

She spent the next two years lecturing on Quimby and in trying to Christianize his faith-cures, by writing comments on his case-book. Meanwhile Quimby died of an ulcer in the stomach in 1866. This year is the date given for the official foundation of Christian Science. One can only conjecture that the reason was that now Quimby was dead, he could no longer dispute Mary Baker Patterson's claim to be the founder of Christian Science.

She began by treating private patients and by lecturing on the art of faith-healing. In 1875 there appeared her world-famous handbook *Science and Health.* Two years later she married Eddy, a business-man, the equable and congenial agent for a firm of sewing-machine manufacturers. Henceforward Christian Science was to stand upon a firm business footing. Mr. Asa Gilbert Eddy saw that the second and third editions of his wife's handbook were protected from literary piracy and thus safeguarded the copyright and the considerable profits. The new ' Bible ' sold for three dollars a copy. Mr. Eddy also introduced his wife to influential persons in Boston, where she lectured. He was her devoted missionary. After these days she never looked back. 668 ' churches ' in

North America acknowledge her as their spiritual leader. She founded a College, an organization with international ramifications, and a famous newspaper, *The Christian Science Monitor*.

She proved herself to be a woman of administrative ability, business acumen and dominating personality. Her logical and speculative abilities were of no mean order, and greatly outran her capacity for literary expression. Her greatest quality was her determination to help to heal the sorrows and ills of mankind, for which she had a deep and lasting sympathy. She rediscovered and expressed in her own character the radiance that should be the distinguishing mark of the Christian life. This frail person was an astonishing example of the triumph of mind over matter until her death of pneumonia in 1910 at the age of eighty-nine.

I

What was the key to her success and what were the benefits of her popular system? She undoubtedly gave a new sense of well-being to multitudes of neurotic and depressed persons. She radiated confidence and thousands of timid, melancholy and self-pitying people regained a sense of cheerful robustness and a faith to live by. It would be less than just to deny the two main values that her creed undoubtedly possessed: in a materialistic age she inculcated a belief in the spiritual interpretation of life, and she rediscovered the Christian art of faith-healing. Her system brought many other benefits also. She restored the notes of health and happiness to the Christian symphony. She effectively repudiated such unworthy notions of God as the belief that all pain is a divine imposition on God's children to teach them resignation. She propagated a profound belief in the goodness of God; so profound, in fact, that she met the age-old problem of evil in a divinely created universe by flatly denying its existence. She and her disciples were motivated by a deep sense of Christian charity. She deserves our gratitude for the happiness she has brought to thousands of mentally sick persons and for the stimulus she has been to the Christian Churches to return to psychological methods of healing.

II

Her system of thought has been summarized by the author herself, as follows:

'First, God is all in all.
Second, God is good, good is mind.
Third, spirit being all, nothing is matter.
Fourth, life, God, omnipotent, good, deny death, evil, sin, disease—
    Disease, sin, evil, death, deny good, omnipotent, God, life.'[2]

It will be immediately apparent that her system is based upon four categorical denials. She denies the existence of matter, pain, evil and death, all four of which historic Christianity is concerned to affirm as having a real existence in time. She declares, 'Matter or body is but a false concept of mortal mind'.[3] It is one thing to say that matter is not eternal; it is quite another to say that it does not exist at all. At the very outset this denial makes absurd the central Christian doctrine, that the Word of God became *flesh* and dwelt among us. Why was she prompted to make this denial contrary to all our human experience? Probably because she thought that the body was the source of all evil; but this is not so—for it is the imagination and the will that are the sources of sinfulness. For the Christian there is nothing evil in matter or in the world, except the misuse which we may make of either. Indeed, our spiritual worth is proven by the way we make use of our bodies.

[2] *Science and Health* (Bird), p. 113.   [3] *ibid.*, p. 413.

In the second place, Mary Baker Eddy denies the existence of pain and sickness. Pain and suffering, she teaches, depend on our foolish belief in matter. She goes so far as to assert:

' A child may have worms, *if you say so*, or any other body.'[4] Absurdity can surely go no further than the following citation from *Science and Health*:

' A boil simply manifests through inflammation and swelling a belief in pain, and this belief is called a boil.'

To this the only appropriate retort is to recite the limerick:

> ' There was a faith-healer of Deal,
> Who said, " Although pain isn't real,
>   When I sit on a pin
>   And it punctures my skin,
> I dislike what I fancy I feel." '

It may readily be granted that pain is often exaggerated: nervous persons and hypochondriacs often imagine they are a prey to a disease which exists only in their fancies. Many people make themselves ill through sheer worrying. But it is totally different to assert that pain in all its forms is sheer illusion. The heart of the Christian Gospel is that we have a suffering Saviour and that by faith in Him we are able to transform suffering into blessing, sin into righteousness, death into eternal life. Our faith is built on that strange Man who hangs upon the Cross. It seems pertinent to ask: How can a faith be Christian, when it denies the reality of the Cross, the acknowledged centre and sign ' of historic Christianity? H. A. L. Fisher says, in the conclusion of *Our New Religion*:

' For the Christian Scientist a brilliant pioneer of drugless healing . . . replaces the suffering figure on the Cross.'

[4] *Science and Health* (Bird), p. 413.

Thirdly, Mrs. Eddy denies the reality of evil and sin. She declares, 'Both sin and sickness are error, and Truth is their remedy.'[5] This denial issues from an honourable determination to 'justify the ways of God to man'. She preserves the unassailable goodness of God by the expedient of denying that sin and evil exist. To assert that sin does not exist, except as an illusion, is virtually to deny the saving work of Christ and to make His sufferings and death mere phantasms. Jesus, on the hypothesis of the Christian Scientists, laboured under the 'delusion' that sin was a reality. Either our Lord's desire to redeem mankind and obtain forgiveness for their sins was an error, or, at least, Jesus came only to prove that our belief in sin was mistaken. By contrast the central tradition of the Christian faith holds that 'all have sinned and fallen short of the glory of God', but that all may be redeemed in Jesus Christ, who has won the final victory over the rebellion of mankind in the Cross and Resurrection, which He communicates to the new People of God, the Christian Church. Christian *realism* is possible, as Dr. Nathaniel Micklem so pertinently remarks, only because the Cross prevents us from shallow optimism and the Resurrection from superficial pessimism. The philosophy (though not necessarily the lives) of Christian Scientists seems, in the absence of the dimension of the Cross, shallow and escapist.

In the fourth place, the existence of death is denied. Mrs. Eddy asserts, 'Life is real and death is an illusion'.[6] Her reasoning seems to be that since we are essentially spiritual and the matter of our bodies is illusory, there is nothing left of us that can die. This, of course, is in open contradiction to the Christian faith which is born out of the Easter experience, when death was not evaded, but conquered by the Risen Lord. Furthermore, this automatic immortality is at variance with the most solemn warnings of our Saviour and His apostles that there is a way of salvation and a way of damnation.

One is bound to admire the logical consistency of Mrs. Eddy

[5] *Science and Health* (Bird), p. 461.   [6] *ibid.*, p. 428.

in her denials, but her life was not consistent with her declared beliefs. For example, she wore artificial teeth and spectacles, showing that her theories did not apply, at least, to diseases of the teeth and the eyes. A more serious inconsistency, however, was publicly revealed in a protest addressed to the trustees of Mrs. Eddy by Mr. John V. Dittemore (a former director of the Mother Church of Christian Science), in which he wrote:

' As you will know, Mrs. Eddy employed physicians professionally, and took drugs on numerous occasions during the last ten years of her life.'[7]

Her philosophy of life also falls under censure for serious misrepresentation of Christian doctrine in two important respects; namely, her teaching about the personality of God and of Jesus Christ. Her God is impersonal, for

' Life, truth and love constitute the triune God, or triple Divine principle.'[8]

That she does not accept the Christian doctrine of the Holy Trinity appears from her avowal:

' The theory of three persons in one God (that is, a personal Trinity or Tri-unity) suggests heathen gods.'[9]

In fact, she invites us to believe in the impossible—an impersonal principle with personal attributes such as love.

Her account of Jesus Christ is equally unorthodox. She revives that most ancient of heresies, Docetism, in denying the reality of our Lord's human nature:

' Wearing in part a human form (that is, as it seemed to

[7] Reported in *The Christian World*, Feb. 28, 1929, and cited in Leslie D. Weatherhead, *Psychology in the Service of the Soul* (Epworth, 1949), p. 219.
[8] *Science and Health* (Bird), p. 277.
[9] *ibid.*, p. 152.

human view), being conceived by a human mother, Jesus was a Mediator between the Spirit and flesh, between Truth and error.'[10]

She further denies that Jesus died by crucifixion. In her volume, *Miscellany*, she speaks of 'the supposedly crucified Christ', and interprets Romans 5.10 as meaning 'for when we were enemies, we were reconciled by the *seeming* death of Christ'. Her claim to have surpassed the apostles in her understanding of the mission of Christ is contained in the following citation:

> 'Jesus' students, not sufficiently advanced to fully understand their Master's triumph, did not perform many wonderful works until they saw Him after His crucifixion, and learned that He had not died.'[11]

But she approaches blasphemy when she declares of Jesus:

> 'Had wisdom characterized all His sayings, He would not have prophesied His own death and thereby hastened or caused it.'[12]

A denial of the reality of the Incarnation, the Cross and the Resurrection of Jesus Christ refutes entirely the claim that her system is a *Christian Science*.

III

Apart from these serious distortions and denials of the Christian message, Christian Science must be accounted dangerous for other reasons. Many lives have been lost through the inability of Mrs. Baker Eddy to distinguish be-

[10] *Science and Health* (Bird), p. 211.
[11] *ibid.*, p. 45.
[12] Cited L. D. Weatherhead, *City Temple Tidings*, Nov. 1950, p. 259.

tween illness caused by germ invasion and illness caused by psychological factors. H. A. L. Fisher avers in *Our New Religion* that the refusal of Christian Scientists to co-operate with members of the medical professions lays them open to the charge of being murderers. It is certain, at least, that they are parasites living upon the precautions of preventive medicine and public health. Furthermore, it is significant that although Christian Science has vast funds, opulent premises and enthusiastic workers, it is never found bringing its mission of health and happiness to the slums. Finally, it can fairly be accused of making religion a means to an end, for God is the means and the end is man's physical well-being. Like Spiritualism it must be accounted a 'Glory for me' and not a 'Glory for God' religion.

IV

These defects in the Christian Science system should make Christians all the more sensible of the greatness of the truth as it is in Christ Jesus. Its realism urges not an evasion of sin, suffering and death, but an attack upon them. A Christian is a follower of a Lord who said : 'In the world ye shall have tribulation, but be of good cheer, I have overcome the world.'

Further, the Gospel moves in a bracing, Christian Science in a relaxed, atmosphere. Jesus said, 'If any man will come after me, let him . . . take up his cross and follow me'. Mary Baker Eddy says, in effect, 'I invite you to a Christianity without tears'. But that cannot be! Christianity is only for those who offer the tears of repentance, who, like Peter, weep bitterly when they hear the cock crow, and remember their broken promises. It is a religion that speaks loudest in sighs, such as Mary's when she lamented, 'They have taken away my Lord and I know not where they have laid Him'. Christianity offers a God who shall wipe away all tears. It is the divine answer to all our human sobbing—to the sobbing of the sinner, the sufferer and the bereft. If we are told that these experiences are unreal, we can only reply that the Christian Scientists are tone-deaf to the tragic notes of our human symphony. Life's foes demand to be faced with bracing realism, not evaded by Christian Science's escapism.

Christian Science is, in fact, a misnomer. It is neither Christian nor scientific. Mary Baker Eddy's cures are remembered, and rightly, with gratitude; her four casualties should not be forgotten—her three husbands and herself.

IV

SPIRITISM

Try the spirits whether they be of God. (I John 4.1)

I

SPIRITISM, the belief that the spirits of the departed actually communicate with the living, is often erroneously styled *Spiritualism*, but Christians repudiate this claim to spirituality on the part of a cult which uses material proofs. How can the attraction that Spiritism has for its devotees be accounted for? It is suggested that three factors explain its contemporary allurement.

The first and most important factor is the deep longing of the bereaved human heart to know whether its beloved dead survive in another world. It is the men and women who sigh, 'O for the touch of a vanished hand and the sound of a voice that is still', who go to spiritistic seances. It is no cause for wonderment that Spiritism should flourish in an age which has seen two major world wars in three decades. For the attitude of distracted persons twice bereaved in a life-time one can have no scorn, but only a profound sympathy.

The second reason for the success of this cult is that three figures of national importance in Great Britain were avowed Spiritists; namely, Sir Arthur Conan Doyle (distinguished novelist and creator of 'Sherlock Holmes', the father of an impressive progeny of literary detectives), Sir Oliver Lodge and Sir William Crookes, the eminent scientists. Spiritism's most renowned contemporary champion is Lord Dowding, former Chief of the Royal Air Force. These men gave to

Spiritism the appearance of being a trustworthy creed because they subscribed to it. At the same time, it should not be forgotten that Sir Oliver Lodge condemned much Spiritism as quackery and superstition. It should also be remembered that a man who is an expert in the physical sciences is not thereby automatically qualified as an expert in the spiritual world.

Success has come to Spiritism for a third reason; because many people are under the impression that it is a form of Christianity, owning an allegiance to Jesus Christ. Such confusion was to be expected (possibly was actually encouraged) when the Spiritist assemblies met in buildings with such names as 'The Church of Christian Fellowship', 'The Temple of the Holy Trinity', or 'The Church of the Spirit'. Despite some similarities in teaching, however, it will be seen that there are wide differences between Christianity and Spiritism.

Though this cult has a modern flavour, it has an ancient lineage. In one sense it might be described as a refined form of ancestor worship. It can be traced back to the most primitive form of religion—animism, which attributed souls or spirits to trees, streams and stones. In the dawn of civilization it was customary to explain the eerie and unaccountable phenomena by reference to the visitation of the spirits of the dead. It was fear-engirded and only a man as desperate as Saul resorted to the witch of Endor to conjure up the dead. The subject was regarded with awesome dread: it was thought to be dangerous and even demonic. The practice was forbidden in the Old Testament and declared to be against the will of God.

Modern Spiritism originated in 1847 in Hydeville in the State of New York, with the announcement that strange revelations through mysterious noises and rappings had been made to Margaret and Kate Fox, children of twelve and nine years, respectively. The children claimed that the spirits sent them messages in answer to their questions in a type of code. Three raps were interpreted as an affirmative answer, one rap as a negative, and two raps as doubtful. The children were

44 CHRISTIAN DEVIATIONS

pronounced to be 'mediums' and from widespread interest in their supposed achievements arose the multiplication of arranged sittings or seances which are the recognized methods of organizing Spiritist meetings to-day. As a result many mediums took up the occult as a lucrative profession and brought the subject into disrepute. A more important result, however, was the foundation of an important body of sincere scientific investigators in 1882, *The Society for Psychical Research*. The proceedings of this society constitute a most impressive examination of all Spiritist claims. They have established the existence of some remarkable phenomena, but the interpretation of these experiences is inconclusive.

II

In justice to Spiritism it must be acknowledged that its teaching and Christianity have a considerable area of common ground. Both agree that man is not simply a complicated body; both hold, in fact, that man is a soul and a body. Moreover, both parties are agreed that individuality survives the disintegration of the body and continues to exercise its faculties. Also, both agree that the resurrection of Jesus Christ is a reality of profound significance.

Furthermore, Spiritists have emphasized that love is the sole and triumphant operative power in the universe, a belief which is closely akin to the Christian claim that God is wholly love. In addition, there is a close affinity between the teaching of Spiritism and the article of the Apostles Creed which Christians profess: 'I believe in the Communion of Saints.' In face of contemporary materialism, atheism and agnosticism the importance of these common tenets is considerable and to this extent Spiritism and Christianity can be regarded as allies. But there are areas of complete divergence which must now be considered.

III

What, then, are these differences and are they important? In general, the differences are both in the manner the information is obtained and in the character and quality of that information.

Christianity believes that man is both spiritual and physical. The doctrine is derived by Christians partly from philosophy but mainly from the life and teaching of Jesus Christ. Christianity's belief in a future life is founded upon God's mighty act in raising Jesus Christ from the grave and upon our Lord's promise, ' If I live, ye shall live also '.

The Spiritists claim that their information on survival after death and the nature of the after-life is received from the dead themselves; that is, from controls who are supposed to transmit their messages through a medium in a trance in the darkness. This claim, however, cannot admit of proof by its very nature. The dilemma has been admirably stated by Dr. Glen Atkins thus:

' On the one hand, only those things which are utterly *unknown* to the living anywhere can be finally and conclusively a testimony to communications from the dead. On the other hand, unless the information thus received is *known* to the living, its truth or falsity can never be proved or disproved.'[1]

Furthermore, the mediums who claim to be in touch with the spirits ' on the other side ' are not conspicuously intelligent. Even Sir Oliver Lodge reluctantly describes them as generally ' not particularly able or highly educated folk '. Dr. James Black evinces a Christian's bewilderment at this fact, as follows:

' With the best will in the world, I cannot understand why

[1] *Modern Religious Cults and Movements* (Allen and Unwin), p. 313.

spirits, presumably purified from the clogging influences of the body, should choose to manifest themselves only or mainly to people of this order. If they manifested themselves to saintly souls or to those who live on a high spiritual and mental level, I could at once appreciate this. . . . Frankly I am puzzled and disturbed by it. God has always chosen the finest instruments to proclaim His finest message.'[2]

By contrast, our information as Christians is received through faith in a Master of Life, whose words we can challenge, and whose character and teaching force us to admit by their quality that they are a revelation of God's very nature. The information of Spiritists is obtained from a stranger of whom they know nothing, through the offices of a medium about whom they know next to nothing.

The second divergence between Spiritism and Christianity is seen in the nature of that future life which both systems depict. Spiritists, moreover, claim that the future life is the prerogative of man, simply as man. The Christian, however, claims that God alone is immortal and that He confers the privilege of eternal life with Him only on those who have tried to do His will. Spiritists believe in an automatic future life: Christians believe in eternal life that God alone can give out of His grace. For this eternal life the individual must fulfil certain moral and spiritual conditions. Christians find it hard to believe that every blackguard after his life is over finds immediate entry into God's holy presence. Nor do they believe that God can be uninterested in the difference between right and wrong. Such a conception is impossibly sentimental for them because they believe that the Judge of all the earth is just.

Furthermore, as will be seen later, the Spiritist's picture of life after death is spiritually superficial and tawdry, compared with the richly meaningful Christian conception of eternity. Christians must repudiate any conception of the

[2] *New Forms of the Old Faith* (Nelson, 1948), pp. 90-1.

after-life which regards it essentially as an automatic rest-cure
and not primarily as the blessedness of everlasting fellowship
with God and His saints. These are real differences and we
injure our holy faith if we attempt to gloss them over.

IV

The Christian criticism of Spiritism makes eight serious
charges against it, now to be detailed. The first accusation is
that Spiritism is frequently a selfish philosophy of life. It
encourages adherents to join its ranks for what they can get out
of it. In Bede Frost's pointed epigram, it is a ' glory for me,
not a glory for God religion '. It tries to satisfy the personal
craving for certainty in spiritual things. It also appeals to the
natural man's desire for a heavenly superannuation on easy
terms. It is too comfortable a religion: it is, in short, Christianity without the Cross. It does not encourage service for
others, nor does it issue a challenge to rebuild the world after
God's heart. It appeals not to the heroic motives, but to man's
desire for security. For our Lord's advice, ' He that loseth his
life shall save it ', it substitutes the tame motto of ' Safety
First '.

The superiority of the Christian faith is seen in the fact
that Jesus appeals to both motives. He who said, ' Come unto
me all ye that labour and are heavy-laden, and I will give you
rest ', also said, ' He that would come after Me, let him take
up his cross and follow Me '. It is true that He promised that
His followers should reign with Him in everlasting life, but
St. Paul is true to His Master in declaring, ' Those who suffer
with Him shall also reign with Him '. Spiritism offers
security, but at too cheap a price. Victory is promised, but
without the triumph of a successful struggle. Those who are
not spiritual invalids and those who are dissatisfied with the
world as it is and wish to remould it, prefer the invigoration
of fighting behind the Cross of Christ.

Despite its preferred name of ' Spiritualism ', Spiritism is often a materialistic religion. This is Christianity's second censure against it. What is so disappointing about Spiritism is the utterly terrestrial nature of the heaven it offers. Heaven is pictured in purely physical terms; it is imagined as a celestial garden city with all the modern conveniences. Should the reader think that this is a gross exaggeration, let him mark the following words which are a record of what the control, Pheneas, is supposed to have told Lady Conan Doyle:

> ' Your home in the other world is ready for you. There is a round small building in the grounds which is filled with exquisite coloured vibrations into which you go when you want your soul's rejuvenation. . . . There is an oblong pond round which coloured birds come to drink.'

' Coloured vibrations ', the reader will note, are bodily sensations—pleasant to the eye and tingling to the spine. But what have such sensory impressions to do with the soul?

Revelations received from other mediums only confirm the impression that this heaven of the Spiritists is the projection of tired spirits in search of a spa and a pump-room. The following excerpt, extracted from the Handbook to Heaven entitled *Spirit Intercourse*, is sufficient evidence for the charge:

> ' Summer land is 1,350 miles from the earth; light, 100-110 degrees. Pet animals and birds numerous. Flowers and fruit in rich abundance; habitations of brick and stone interspersed with gardens.'

The other advantages are left to our imagination to depict. In the same vein the catalogue might be continued to include comfortably furnished apartments, with electricity, hot and cold water, and all the usual conveniences. If that is heaven, one can as easily imagine a sprightly St. Peter as receptionist, walking down a spiral staircase in spats, wearing immaculate morning-dress, with a carnation in his button-hole and a watch-chain on which hangs a bunch of golden keys! This uncelestial cavalcade will not do for Christians. Men and women could be gulled by such a materialist picture of heaven only because they have never understood the meaning of eternal life as it is declared by Christ. Otherwise, they would have rejected so spurious an imitation. The Spiritist after-life is too like Valhalla or the Paradise of fleshly Moslem expectation.

The third charge against Spiritism is that its revelation is untheological—it tells us nothing about God. It seems that communion with God is nowhere envisaged. In fact, God seems to the Spiritists to be entirely uninterested in man, and man's interest in God is purely speculative. It is not too much to say with Dr. James Black 'the one thing that Spiritualism lacks is the "spiritual"'.[3] The paucity of references to God in the communications of the controls might lead one to believe that God is entirely an afterthought, instead of being the only conceivable ground and guarantee of the survival of the soul beyond death.

The fourth charge against Spiritism is that it can be a dangerous faith. It is not denied that spirits might have intercourse with human beings. The Bible, in fact, clearly asserts that there are two kinds of spirits—good and evil. Believers are warned, 'Try the spirits, whether they be of God'. And, in this connection, Spiritists themselves admit not only that frauds have taken place in seances, but that evil spirits are occasionally present. The following warning is taken from a book written by a psychic medium, who herself exercised a spiritist practice for over twenty years. The book is *Voices from the Void* and its author is Mrs. Travers Smith (or, Hesther Dowden, her maiden name).

'If I may venture to advise persons who long to speak once more with persons who have vanished into darkness, I should say it is wise and sane not to make the attempt. The chances against genuine communication are about ten

[3] *New Forms of the Old Faith* (Nelson, 1948), p. 103.

D

to one: the disappointments and doubts connected with the experiments are great.'

Her *caveat* was repeated in a book she published in 1920. There can be no doubt that occult trafficking is dangerous for anxious, excitable and neurotic people, and such investigation should be left in the hands of the accredited societies engaged in psychic experiments. Spiritism is not only dangerous to sanity, it is also a menace to faith. Professor Grensted offers this wise advice:

'The traffic in signs, the miracle-mongering not for the sake of love but for the sake of the miracle, the quest for manifestations and the rest, can become a most perilous distraction, separating the Spirit alike from God and from the everyday world in which God's work must be done.'[4]

At heart Spiritism is not trust in God; it is born of distrust of Him. It is an attempt to substitute experimental certainty for faith. It is the monstrous design to subject God to the indignity of a test-tube examination. It should be repudiated, as our Lord repudiated the Evil One: 'Thou shalt not tempt the Lord Thy God.'

Our Saviour continually warned His disciples against those who wanted 'signs' or positive demonstrations and who refused to take anything on trust. 'This wicked and adulterous generation seeketh a sign, but it shall not be given unto it.' Our Lord showed in the Parable of Dives and Lazarus that no messages from the dead can supplant or confirm a living faith. Jesus depicts the rich man asking that a messenger be sent to his brothers on earth to warn them about the reality of the future life. But the answer was given, 'They have Moses and the prophets; let them hear them. . . . If they hear not Moses and the prophets, neither will they be persuaded, though one rose from the dead.' St. Paul plainly re-issued the warning when he counselled Timothy: 'But the Spirit plainly

[4] Article, *Expository Times*, Vol. LIV, p. 203.

saith that in after times some will fall away from the faith, giving heed to deceiving spirits, and teaching of demons, through the impostures of those who speak falsely, men seared in their own consciences.'

Spiritism's success should be a warning to all faithful Christians that when the Christian faith in God and knowledge of God is diluted, vapid and vague, then pale imitations of the original find a ready market amongst the credulous.

The sixth count against Spiritism is that its claims are inconclusive. While it may be admitted that the Spiritists present us with phenomena which transcend our normal experience, it cannot be accepted that the only explanation for these is the agency of departed spirits. At least four explanations have been offered to account for these phenomena. Some have attributed them to fraud. Others have said that they are self-deception—the unintended giving away of personal information to the medium or a temporary lapse in concentration of observation on the part of the person attending a seance. Others, again, have attributed it to a collective unconsciousness into which the medium delves. A most promising alternative explanation connects the phenomena with telepathy—the communication of thoughts from one mind to another bypassing the usual five senses. Roman Catholics, for their part, urge that all the spirits taking part in the seances are evil spirits. Amid this variety of explanations, the only verdict on the Spiritist claims must be that of 'Not proven'.

The seventh charge against Spiritism is that it is unnecessary. A spiritual faith is in no need of physical attestation. Belief in the future life after death of human souls does not rest on miraculous testimony but on our faith in the character and fidelity and promises of the God and Father of the Risen Christ. Spiritism is therefore otiose.

The eighth and final charge against Spiritism is that it contains elements of the suspicious and the ridiculous. Seance rooms hold their proceedings in darkness, preventing any possibility of seeing and examining the evidence; there is an entire absence of normal control; and even the 'temperamental' nature of some mediums is bound to lend suspicion to seances. G. K. Chesterton has satirized the element of the ridiculous in his sceptical question: 'Do you expect to hear the voice of God calling from a coal-cellar?' The answer is that God's voice is heard saying of Jesus, 'This is My beloved Son: hear ye Him.' And that beloved Son has said simply, 'In My Father's house are many mansions. I go to prepare a place for you. If it were not so, I would have told you.' Trusting Him, the first-born from the dead, we take His promise on trust. Experiments are unnecessary where faith prevails.

> I know not where His islands lift
> Their fronded palms in air;
> I only know I cannot drift
> Beyond His love and care.

That is all we know and all we need to know. A spiritual faith cannot rest on materialistic proofs. The sole foundation for our belief in eternity as Christians must be God's promise and 'the exceeding greatness of His power to usward who believe, according to the working of the strength of His might, which He wrought in Christ when He raised Him from the dead'.

V

SEVENTH-DAY ADVENTISM

Now therefore why tempt ye God, that ye should put a yoke upon the neck of the disciples, which neither our fathers nor we were able to bear?
(Acts 15.10)

THIS millenarian sect, which flourishes among uneducated and underprivileged peoples and classes, claims that it is the only true Church because it alone keeps the fourth Commandment inviolate by observing the Sabbath on the seventh day, whereas the rest of Christendom observes it on the first day of the week. Its followers, the Seventh-Day Adventists declare, alone will be among the 144,000 elect who will attain to everlasting life.

How then, does such an odd creed commend itself to hundreds of thousands of adherents? In the first place, it has an army of aggressive evangelists; it does not, like so many Churches, leave witnessing to the professionals. These evangelists would shame most Christians by their thorough, if literal, acquaintance with the Bible, which they are able to quote volubly, with references to chapter and verse. Even their Adventism, despite the crudity of some of its teaching, represents a two-fold protest against both the modernism that teaches an inevitable progress towards Utopia and the less refined traditionalism that clings to a belief in a Hell where the damned suffer everlasting torments. In opposition to both of these concepts, Seventh-Day Adventism declares that the Second Advent will take place quietly (no blood-curdling Armageddon will bring the new world order in) and that evildoers will be annihilated, not subjected to eternal tortures. These factors account, at least partially, for the numerical success of this sect which originated, like so many others, in the United States of America in the nineteenth century.

I

The movement cannot be understood apart from a brief account of its history. As in the case of Christian Science and Theosophy, Seventh-Day Adventism had a female founder, Ellen Harmon, though she is better known under her married name, as Mrs. Ellen White. She shares with Mrs. Mary Baker Eddy another peculiarity—she did not admit her theological thefts! Just as Mrs. Eddy leaned heavily upon the teaching of the quack Quimby, without acknowledging her indebtedness, so did Mrs. White pick the brains of William Miller, the founder of the Adventists.

William Miller was a Baptist, born at Pittsfield, Massachusetts, in 1782, who was educated at Low Hampton in New York State. This farmer studied the Bible with extraordinary zeal, but without historical knowledge or critical acumen, and announced in 1831 that he had discovered the exact date of Christ's Second Coming. He declared confidently that, on the basis of the predictions of Daniel and Revelation, this event would take place in 1843. When nothing happened during this year, he admitted a mistake in his calculations and postponed the fulfilment of his prophecy to the following year. When he was again proved wrong, he gave up Adventism. In his significant renunciation, he stated:

'On the passing of the published time, I frankly acknowledged my disappointment. We expected the personal coming of Christ at that time; and now to contend that we were not mistaken is dishonest. We should never be ashamed frankly to confess our errors. I have no confidence in any of the new theories that grew out of that movement, namely, that Christ then came as the Bridegroom, that the door of mercy was closed, that there is no salvation for sinners, that the seventh trumpet then sounded, or that it was a fulfilment of prophecy in any sense.'[1]

Despite his recantation, Ellen Harmon (White) a neurotic young woman, persisted in believing that his prophecies were substantially correct, and founded a sect, named the Seventh-Day Adventists. They held the view that

' the Lord did really come in 1844, not to the earth, but to cleanse the sanctuary in Heaven. . . . The Lord passed into the sanctuary in 1844, which Mrs. White was taken up to Heaven and shown.'[2]

They believed that our Lord then cleansed the sanctuary and commenced the Final Judgment, closing the door of mercy to sinners. They claimed that only those who knew about the ' change' could benefit by His mediation. Others, according to Ellen White, ' offer up their useless prayers to the apartment which Jesus left '.[3] Salvation was made to depend on knowledge of an event in 1844 of which only the Seventh-Day Adventists had heard, and upon the observance of the Jewish Sabbath in place of the Christian Lord's Day. The latter tradition of Christendom is named ' The Mark of the Beast' by Seventh-Day Adventists. Their greatest claim is that they are alone in preaching the three messages referred to in Revelation 14.6-12, that ' the seal of God is the holy Sabbath' and that the 144,000 of Revelation 7.1-8, who are to be translated at the Advent, are now being sealed.

II

The peculiar beliefs of the Seventh-Day Adventists must now be considered in detail. The first feature is, of course,

[1] *History of the Advent Message*, pp. 410, 412.
[2] *Early Writings*, pp. 114-15.   [3] *Spiritual Gifts*, p. 172.

their teaching on Adventism. Now, although the founder of the Adventist movement, William Miller, admitted that his predictions had been erroneous, Mrs. White refused to give up the idea of a predicted Advent. Mr. D. M. Canright, a former elder of the sect, informs us in his *Seventh-Day Adventism Renounced* that he was taught that ' the Judgment of the World had started already in 1844, and that the End of the World was to be expected in this generation '.

The assertion that Christ entered into the sanctuary of Heaven to effect its cleansing was the doctrine discovered by Mrs. White which gave a significance to the year 1844. This, however, was done only at the cost of a severe distortion of the New Testament teaching on the Atonement. She held that the work of our Lord was not finished on earth in the days of His Passion, because ' as the closing portion of His work as priest, before He takes His throne as King, He will make the great atonement '.[4] According to her, Christ entered only the outer sanctuary at the Ascension, not the holy of holies, although this is clearly contradicted by Hebrews 1.3.

The third and most prominent element in their teaching is the insistence upon a seventh-day Sabbath. This position they defend on Biblical and historical grounds. While Mrs. Ellen White admitted that the New Covenant had done away with the Old Covenant of Moses, she yet held that the moral, as distinct from the ceremonial precepts of the Law were still binding on Christians. She went on to argue that since the observance of the Sabbath on the seventh day occurs as one of the commandments of the moral law, therefore the observance of the Sabbath on the seventh day is unrepealed and is a perpetual obligation on Christians. To substantiate this teaching, Mrs. White claimed to have had a vision of the sanctuary in Heaven where

' Jesus raised the cover of the ark, and she beheld the tables of stone on which the ten commandments were written. She was amazed as she saw the Fourth Commandment in the

[4] *Fundamental Principles.*

very centre of the ten precepts, with a soft halo of light encircling it.'[5]

The historical claim of the Seventh-Day Adventists that the Churches fell into apostasy in this matter rests on the assertion that the Council of Laodicea in A.D. 364 changed the Sabbath or seventh day to Sunday or the first day of the week.

They further teach that Jesus Christ inherited a fallen human nature, as may be gathered from the following citation:

'In His humanity Christ partook of our sinful, fallen nature. If not, then He was not "made like unto us His brethren", was not "in all points tempted like as we are", did not overcome as we have to overcome, and is not therefore, the complete and perfect Saviour man needs and must have to be saved.'[6]

Their final distinctive doctrine is their belief in the sleep of the soul after death. The state of the dead is said to be 'one of silence, inactivity and entire unconsciousness'. The five proof texts for this doctrine, all significantly taken from the Old Testament, are: Psalm 146.4; Eccl. 9.5,6,10; Dan. 12.2.

III

Seventh-Day Adventism must now be subjected to detailed criticism, the thoroughness of which is warranted only by its rapid spread and its tendency to insinuate itself by glossing over the differences between its tenets and those of the historic Christian Churches.

This sect lacks the charity which should characterize the company of those to whom Christ addressed the words, 'I

---

[5] Cited W. C. Irvine, *Heresies Exposed* (Pickering and Inglis, 8th edn., 1937), p. 149.
[6] *Bible Readings for the Home Circle* (1915 edn.), p. 115.

have called you friends, not servants'. None the less, the Seventh-Day Adventists acknowledge themselves alone to be among the 144,000 elect and castigate all the Churches which celebrate the Lord's Day on the first day of the week (the rest of Christendom, no less) as 'Babylon', bearing 'the mark of the Beast'.

Their insistence upon the necessity for keeping the seventh day or Jewish Sabbath as one of the main articles of faith on which salvation depends is both foreign to the New Testament in its declension from grace to legalism and deficient in any true sense of Christian proportion. Furthermore, its assertion that the change from the seventh day Sabbath to the first day Sunday was made by the Council of Laodicea is unhistorical.

Col. 2.14 rightly reminds us that 'the hand-writing of ordinances' (the Law of Moses) was 'blotted out' and nailed to Christ's Cross, as in ancient times old bills were nailed to the doorpost when paid. Since Christ has met every claim of the Law on our behalf, its precepts are no longer obligatory on Christians. The distinction which Mrs. White made between ceremonial and moral law is entirely unknown in the Old Testament, as a perusal of Ex. 24.3 will show conclusively. Furthermore, it is difficult to understand how she could have regarded the matter of observing a particular day as more holy than another as a moral issue, when it is more obviously a matter of ceremonial import. In any case, Christians believe in the supremacy of grace over law, whereas she would make the New Testament a new Leviticus. The New Testament shows us that even the moral law of the Old Testament is superseded. The Old Testament declares 'Thou shalt not kill'. But this negative precept is replaced in the New Testament by the more positive and penetrating counsel, 'If thine enemy hunger, feed him; if he thirst, give him drink'.

The grace of our Lord Jesus Christ frees us from empty ceremonial and scrupulous adherence to the letter of the Law. St. Augustine insisted that all the ethical precepts of Christianity could be summed up in the injunction: 'Love God and do what you like.' In short, this doctrine of the Seventh-Day Adventists is an irrelevant legalism in the life of the Spirit. It is already condemned in the words of Col. 2.16-17, ' Let no man therefore judge you in meat, or in drink, or in respect of an holy day, or of the new moon, or of the sabbath days: Which are a shadow of things to come; but the body is of Christ.'

There is, moreover, a positive reason for the change from the seventh day to the first for the celebration of the Lord's Day during the Christian dispensation. The old Sabbath was a memorial of the origin of life; the new Sabbath, commemorating Christ's resurrection, is a memorial of the victory of life over death. In the felicitous words of Dr. Lewis Radford:

> ' The old Sabbath marked the close of the first stage of divine activity, Creation; the new Lord's Day marks the beginning of the second stage, Regeneration. The Sabbath ended the week with a *Nunc Dimittis* of resignation; the Lord's Day begins the week with a *Te Deum* of renewal.'[7]

Even the claim that the Council of Laodicea introduced the change from the celebration of the Jewish Sabbath to the Christian Lord's Day is unwarranted. In the first place, this was an Eastern Council and was therefore not authoritative for the more important Western Churches. In the second place, it merely forbade Christians from abstaining from work on the Jewish Sabbath, calling this practice ' Judaising'. In fact, there is evidence to show that the Lord's Day was generally celebrated on the first day of the week in the second century. *The Epistle to Barnabas* (early second century) records: ' Wherefore, also, we keep the eighth day with joyfulness, the day also on which Jesus rose from the dead.' And Justin Martyr, writing about the middle of the second century, declares: ' But Sunday is the day on which we all hold a com-

[7] L. B. Radford, *Ancient Heresies in Modern Dress* (Robertson, Melbourne, 1913), p. 78.

mon assembly, because it is the first day of the week on which God . . . made the world; and Jesus Christ our Saviour on the same day rose from the dead.'

The most overwhelming indictment of the sabbatarianism of this sect is offered by Dr. James Black:

'To found a church on that ancient, outlived and outdated Jewish Sabbath passes comprehension. There are so many big things worth fighting for. Why fight for a shadow?'[8]

Our third criticism must be of the Adventism of the sect. Their system is vitiated by a misconception of the function of prophecy. They assume that the prophet's task is to foretell the course of events like an inspired crystal-gazer. Beyond the immediate horizon of the prophet there is only the vision of the final victory of the Kingdom of God. The prophet tells of the consequence of unrighteousness and predicts the joy of the people of God if they repent, but he does not predict events in detail. If he did, this would make his offer of salvation to be freely accepted meaningless, for a predetermined future and an appeal to change the heart are incompatible. In any case, the Seventh-Day Adventists go beyond the statement of our Lord in their arrogance, for He declared of the Second Advent, 'No man knoweth the hour, . . . not even the Son'. Seventh-Day Adventists presumably lay claim to a higher revelation than that vouchsafed to the Messiah.

Fourthly, the Seventh-Day Adventists in their doctrine of the sanctuary would destroy the true significance of the Ascension of our Lord and of His Priesthood. They claim that there were two stages in our Lord's High Priesthood, corresponding to the Jewish high priest's ministrations first in the outer chamber and then in the inner chamber of the earthly tabernacle. But the Epistle to the Hebrews represents Jesus as entering into the inmost sanctuary of the presence of God, not merely to purify the heavenly things, but 'now to appear be-

[8] *New Forms of the Old Faith* (Nelson, 1948), p. 221.

fore the face of God for us '.[9] In the New Testament purify-
ing and appearing are clearly two aspects of the one fact.
Adventists have, therefore, no shred of Biblical evidence for
their fantastic belief that the appearance of the perfect Man
to present His sacrifice of obedience even unto death took
place in A.D. 1844. The writer of Hebrews believed that it took
place at the Ascension.[10]

Dr. Radford draws out the logical consequences of this
belief, with its denial of the New Testament doctrine that
Christ 'ever liveth to make intercession for us', in the
comment:

'Adventism stands committed to the amazing theory that
for eighteen centuries the ascended Christ was still waiting
to enter the sanctuary of the presence of God and to prepare
the heavenly world for the approach of man to God. . . .
If this atoning entry took place in 1844, what was the scene,
the character, the efficacy of His activity for those eighteen
centuries of human time? '[11]

The effect of this belief is also to reduce the function of the
Holy Spirit during eighteen centuries to being the minister
of the unfinished work of the Father and the Son.

The assertion that the intermediate state after death is
one of entire unconsciousness can find Old Testament war-
rants, but is entirely contradicted by the New Testament.
The latter teaches or implies that the soul is conscious in the
unseen world. The parable of Lazarus (Luke 16.22-5), the
promise our Lord made to the dying thief (Luke 23.43), the
impatient cry of the waiting martyrs (Rev. 6.9-11), the wish of
St. Paul (Phil. 1.21), and the missionary activity of the human
spirit of the Christ among the departed between His death
and His resurrection (I Pet. 3.19 and 4.6) controvert the assertions of the Seventh-Day Adventists.

Finally, their admittedly erroneous interpretations in the

[9] Heb. 9.24.   [10] Heb. 8.1.
[11] *Ancient Heresies in Modern Dress* (Robertson, 1913), p. 87.

past awaken grave suspicions and leave little room for confidence in their doctrines. On two occasions their predictions of the Second Advent have been proved false. They once began their Sabbath at six in the evening, but changed the time when they discovered that the Biblical Sabbath began at sunset. There was a time when they enforced a vegetarian diet on their adherents; once they condemned all religious organization and political voting as 'marks of the Beast'; once they prevented their children from attending and being contaminated by State schools. None of these practices is now insisted upon. Their official explanation that the Lord was trying their faith by disappointments was convenient, but it is not convincing.

On the whole, then, their claims prove that their distinctive doctrines are merely the products of computation and speculation. They have no New Testament warrant and they deserve to be designated both heretical and schismatical. These labels will not disturb them in the least, for they have already anathematized all other Christian denominations as 'The Whore of Babylon', since they do not imitate their Judaistic Sabbatarianism; but they will serve to put Christians on their guard against accepting the claims of the Seventh-Day Adventists. Yet more orthodox Christians would do well to imitate their warm missionary generosity, which speaks of grace in practice, despite their cold legalistic theology.

VI

JEHOVAH'S WITNESSES

*But now abideth faith, hope and charity; and the
greatest of these is charity.* (I Cor. 13.13)

JEHOVAH'S WITNESSES is the final name chosen by a sect
which has been known variously as 'The Millennial Dawn',
'The International Bible Students Association', 'The Watch-
tower Organization', and the company of those who subscribe
to the doctrine 'Millions now living will never die!' The
present designation of this body was applied to it by 'Judge'
Rutherford in 1931 and is based upon the words of Isaiah,
'Ye are my witnesses, saith Jehovah'.[1] This prolific sect has
come into the public eye by reason of its pertinacious tract-
sellers and because its adherents refuse to undergo conscrip-
tion or military service.

I

It originated in the mind of Charles Taze Russell at Alle-
ghany, Pittsburgh in 1872. Its author, then aged twenty, was
a member of the local Congregational Church and of the
Y.M.C.A. in the neighbourhood. The real forerunners of the
movement, however, were a group of Second Adventists, and,
in particular, a J. H. Paton to whose writings Russell was
greatly indebted, though it was beneath him to acknowledge
this.

Russell was a wealthy haberdasher, who had inherited five

[1] Isa. 43.10.

shops from his father, but which he sold in order to devote his entire working days to the dissemination of his views. As a speaker he was compelling, and as an organizer efficient. In 1884 he founded a new religious organization named the Zion's Watch Tower Society. Apart from a magazine which he edited and largely wrote, and a mass of tracts which he composed, he produced a seven volume series entitled *Studies in the Scriptures*, which is the main compendium of the doctrines of the Witnesses. The movement spread to England in 1880 and in a further eight years its representatives were active in China, India, Turkey, Haiti and Africa.

Russell is a curiously disreputable figure to have originated a new religious movement. So overweening was his egotism that he claimed to be a competent Greek scholar, though, as was proved in court, he did not know a letter of the alphabet of that language. His domineering conceit and wayward affections became widely known when his wife sued him for divorce and her petition was readily granted. He was accused by the *Brooklyn Eagle* of selling grain, which he advertised as 'miracle-wheat', at sixty dollars a bushel, and he admitted that there was 'some element of truth' in the charge. He was also believed to have played upon the fears of sick persons to induce them to make over their fortunes to his organization. This was all the more hypocritical of him as he jibed at the monies collected by the Christian Churches and advertised Witness gatherings as 'No Collection Meetings'. His egotism was boundless for he stated in the introductory pages of his *Studies in the Scriptures* that it would be better to leave the Bible unopened and to read his commentary on it, than to omit the latter and read only the Bible.

Russell died in October 1916. So impressed was the attorney of the Witnesses, the misnamed 'Judge' Rutherford, that he wrote:

'When the history of the Church of Christ is fully written, it will be found that the place next to St. Paul in the gallery of fame as expounders of the Gospel of the great Master will be occupied by Charles Taze Russell.'[2]

It is hardly surprising that so ardent a devotee of the founder of the movement should have been elected to succeed him. From 1917 until his death in 1942, Rutherford led the Witnesses with an iron but successful hand. He, too, was a prolific writer and he implemented the propaganda of the organization by a radio network and the sale of gramophone records of his addresses.

Despite its popularity, however, the movement was banned in several countries because its adherents refused the duties of citizenship and proselytized amongst the members of the Christian Churches. They were proscribed in Northern Rhodesia, after a disturbance in the Copper Belt in the nineteen-thirties. In 1940 and 1941 the New Zealand and Australian Governments outlawed them as a subversive organization. In January 1947 the Supreme Court of Canada ruled that they 'were not a religious body' and in the same year they were banned in Southern Rhodesia.

II

One of the main reasons for their success in terms of statistics is their autocratic and hierarchic type of organization. This is marked by all the efficiency characteristic of a modern international business-house. At the head is a central, all-powerful Board of Directors. Under this Board and responsible to it are the various 'Religious Servants' and beneath them the many 'Zone Servants'. The latter have responsibility for the local groups, which are known as 'Companies'. They meet in the 'Kingdom Hall'. At the head of each Company is the 'Service Director', who is responsible to the Zone Servant for running the Company. He is assisted

[2] Cited by H. H. Stroup, *The Jehovah's Witnesses* (Columbia University Press, 1945), pp. 12-13.

E

by a 'service committee' which takes charge of various activities, particularly of the 'back calls', that is, repeated visiting of contacts. Women are discouraged from seeking office and each member of the hieraarchy obeys the orders of his superior without question.

The chief task of the Witnesses is the distribution of the official publications from door to door. Each member is expected to assume his share of these duties and many are equipped with a portable gramophone on which recordings of Rutherford's sermons are played to the householders. All details of visits have to be reported on specially printed forms to the Board of Directors at headquarters. In brief, the Witnesses are organized as a group of religious commercial travellers.

A survey of their teaching will reveal that the Jehovah's Witnesses are heretics, in addition to being schismatics. In their doctrine of God they are monotheistic, if not definitely unitarian. Perhaps their teaching about the person of Christ is most akin to the Arian heresy of the fourth century A.D., for they assert that the Son of God is a created being. This is the purport of the following citation from Russell:

'As he (Jesus) was the highest of all Jehovah's creation, so also was he the first, the direct creation of God, the "only Begotten", and then he, as Jehovah's power, and in his name, created all things. . . .'[3]

Russell repudiates the Chalcedonian Definition's claim that in Jesus Christ the divine and human natures co-existed:

'Neither was Jesus a combination of the two natures, human and spiritual. The blending of two natures produces neither the one nor the other, but an imperfect, hybrid thing, which is obnoxious to the divine arrangement.'[4]

The Witnesses are committed to the curious belief that before

[3] *Studies in the Scriptures,* V, p. 84.   [4] *ibid.,* I, p. 179.

His incarnation Jesus was the Archangel Michael, which they believe is taught in Dan. 12.1. They also hold that Jesus gave up His angelic nature in the days of His flesh and was an ordinary fallible mortal. They claim that, although Jesus was not divine, He paid at His death the ransom necessary to set men free from death, but that His work of Atonement 'will be completed with the close of the Millennial Age'.[5] They further reduce the stature of the eternal Son of God by declaring that elect Christians, 'the little flock', will 'be reckoned as joint sacrificers, joint mediators, joint reconcilers' with Jesus.[6] Salvation largely consists in being imitators of Jesus, which argues, of course, self-salvation.

The Witnesses do not believe that the redeeming work of Christ was completed on the Cross or that those who have faith in Him are saved from their sins and inherit eternal life. Russell taught

'The "ransom for all" given by "the man Christ Jesus" does not give or guarantee everlasting life or blessing to any man; but it does guarantee to every man another opportunity or trial for life everlasting.'[7]

Thus, far from being saved by Christ, each man must work out his own salvation:

'Some have been blinded in part, and some completely, by the God of this world, and they must be recovered from blindness as well as from death, that they, *each for himself*, may have a full chance to prove, by obedience or disobedience, their worthiness or unworthiness of life eternal.'[8]

This is clearly justification by works, not justification by faith. The Witnesses also believe that Jesus was provided with a

[5] J. K. van Baalen, *The Chaos of Cults* (Eerdmans, Grand Rapids, Michigan, 1938), p. 147.
[6] *ibid.*
[7] *Studies in the Scriptures,* I, p. 150.
[8] *ibid.,* I, p. 158.

new spiritual body at the resurrection, and that His human body was neither raised nor glorified. In one place Russell teaches:

' He was put to death *a man*, but was raised from the dead a *spirit being* of the highest order of the divine nature. . . .'[9]

In another he declares:

' Our Lord's human body was, however, supernaturally removed from the tomb; because had it remained there it would have been an insurmountable obstacle to the faith of the disciples, who were not yet instructed in spiritual things. . . .'[10]

Significantly (for the Witnesses are essentially a commercial organization), the permanent status of the Ascended Christ is described as being ' the Chief Executive Officer of Jehovah '[11]

It is not surprising that the Witnesses find the doctrine of the Trinity irrational, since they have reduced the status of the eternal Son of God to that of a fallible mortal and conceive of the Holy Spirit as merely the invisible influence of Jehovah.[12]

They have a ghoulish fondness for the text, ' The wages of sin is death '. They claim that all men are destroyed in death, but that all the dead will be raised again and given a second chance at the Second Advent of Christ. In making such assertions they misread the promise made by our Lord to the penitent thief, ' This day thou shalt be with me in Paradise ', and the implications of the metaphor by which the New Testament describes the dead as those ' that are fallen asleep in Christ '. The doctrine of the second chance is an encouragement to libertarians, apart from its infidelity to the New Testament insistence on the way of salvation and the way of damnation as irrevocable destinies of men. This doctrine

---

[9] *Studies in the Scriptures*, V, p. 453.   [10] *ibid.*, II, p. 129.
[11] Rutherford, *Riches*, p. 94.   [12] *ibid.*, p. 188.

alone gives substance to the taunt that the teaching of the Jehovah's Witnesses is the religion of the natural man. Should evil men refuse the proffered salvation the second time, their fate will be annihilation, not eternal torment or damnation.

Despite the erroneous nature of much of this teaching, the Witnesses can be congratulated on refusing to picture God as a divine sadist, whose dignity is established by the torturing of the damned. Rutherford taught:

> 'Eternal torture is void of the principle of love "God is love". A Creator that would torture His creatures eternally would be a fiend, and not a God of love.'[13]

Furthermore, the Witnesses teach that even death may be spiritually remedial. Their weakness is that they cannot conceive of divine love as *holy* love also: a world without rewards and punishments here and hereafter would be an immoral universe.

The unscriptural speculation of the Witnesses is given full scope in their account of the Second Advent and the Millennium. Russell declared that the Seventh Millennium was the beginning of the Reign of Christ, and he calculated that 1872 was the exact six-thousandth year from the Creation of Adam and Eve. He prophesied that the final end of the world would take place in 1914. Since that time his followers have postponed the date to some time before 1984 when Gabriel's trumpet will blow and Christ will announce that the final end has come. Then God's 'Great Theocracy' will be established on earth and Jehovah's Witnesses will be the only survivors to share in this Divine Kingdom.

Their account of the Millennium is far more detailed than that offered by the Book of Revelation and they have already decided how the problem of feeding the resurrected bodies may be solved:

> 'Remembering the Lord's promise that in the Millenial

[13] *World Distress*, p. 40.

period "the earth shall yield her increase" and that the desert and the wilderness-places of the earth shall become as a Garden of Eden, we may safely estimate upon all the land, which we may find, according to recent estimates, to be 57,000,000 square miles or over 36,000,000,000 acres. What would this mean as to space for each individual who has ever lived in the world, i.e. 28,441,126,838 persons? It means that there would be twelve-hundred and seventy-five acres for each little village of two hundred families. Quite a sufficiency of room, all will agree, under the new conditions promised. But if more space be necessary, with faith we will readily see that it will be quite within the divine power to raise vast continents from the depths of the ocean, or indeed to give a literal as well as a symbolical fulfilment to the declaration—There shall be no more sea.'[14]

The only fitting retort to such speculations is that of Dr. Reinhold Niebuhr's, that faith has nothing to do with either the furniture of heaven or the temperature of hell!

After the battle of Armageddon the 144,000 faithful Jehovah's Witnesses will be taken up into heaven, there to rule with Christ over the new earth, which will be inhabited by the Jonadabs, or people of good will.

In our account of the beliefs of the Witnesses we cannot omit their loveless condemnation of the Christian Churches as devil-controlled. There could be no worse offence against Christian charity than this typical citation from their teaching:

' These facts are set forth here, not for the purpose of holding men up to ridicule, but for the purpose of informing the people that the ecclesiastical systems, Catholic and Protestant, are under supervision and control of the Devil, and form a part of his visible organization, and therefore constitute the anti-Christ.'[15]

A sect claiming to be Christian, yet so vicious in its attitude to

[14] Rutherford, *Riches*, p. 188.   [15] Rutherford, *Deliverance*, p. 222.

others who take the name of Christ on their lips, is guilty of an inner contradiction, for its spirit denies its profession.

In general, Jehovah's Witnesses fall under censure on four main characteristics. First, their doctrine is based upon an arbitrary selection of texts from the Scriptures, but the main body of the teaching of Jesus and His apostles is either evaded or perverted; and to each ounce of the Bible a hundredweight of speculation is added.

In the second place, their doctrine is largely based upon the obscurities of such apocalyptic books as Daniel and Revelation, implying that the Revelation of God is a tangled skein only to be unravelled by the subtle minds of this sect. But Christianity is not a mystery religion for initiates, for we ' have seen the glory of God in the face of Jesus Christ ', who declared ' I am the light of the world '.

Thirdly, the use of the Bible as an *Old Moore's Almanac* of prediction is to misunderstand its purpose and to claim to know more than our Lord Himself who confessed that He did not know the time of the coming of the Son of Man again on the clouds.

Fourthly, their creed must be rejected because it offers salvation on too easy terms, affirming, in effect, that payment for it may be deferred to another existence. This is to repudiate the solemn and urgent either-or of the Bible, and to sentimentalize the conception of a Holy God. Moreover, as we have seen, this is a salvation by good works, not by faith in the victory of Christ.

IV

One further question remains to be answered: How have the devotees of such an unbalanced creed succeeded in winning so many members? This question is merely another way of asking: What can the Churches learn from the strategy of Jehovah's Witnesses?

Russell's success was partly due to his clarity of thought,

simplicity of expression in untechnical language, and abundance of illustrations drawn from everyday life. Further, he and his followers have an unrivalled knowledge of Holy Writ and can quote chapter and verse for their opinions. It has been established that there are over 5,000 different Scriptural citations in the books of Russell.[16] Jehovah's Witnesses have had the wisdom to assume and count upon every member being a propagandist of its organization, using the most up-to-date methods such as gramophone and radios and attractively printed, bound and illustrated volumes.

Even their doctrines, in at least two cases, represent a healthy protest and reaction against current Christian orthodoxy. In their teaching about the 'last things' they refuse to accept the 'fire and brimstone' picture of Hell and rightly protest against a doctrine that envisages punishment as vindictive not remedial. The Jehovah's Witnesses, although denying the responsibilities of citizenship in so many ways, have protested against the devilries of modern warfare and the extravagance of modern life. It is also on record that their egalitarian convictions impelled them to welcome Socialism even in its early days, when few religious folk were Socialists. These, even when we condemn the Jehovah's Witnesses in so much, must be counted as its assets.

[16] cf. Black, *New Forms of the Old Faith* (Nelson, 1948), p. 200.

VII

THE MORMONS

For other foundation can no man lay than that which is laid, which is Jesus Christ. (I Cor. 3.11)

THE MORMONS are so called from the *Book of Mormon*, their official source-book, but prefer to call themselves 'The Church of Jesus Christ of Latter-Day Saints'. This bizarre religious society is found chiefly in the United States of America, but, as it is an efficient proselytizing body, its 900,000 members are found scattered throughout the British Commonwealth and even as far north as Iceland and as far east as China.

Three factors help to account for the remarkable spread of Mormonism. Chief of these is its militant missionary spirit, which was first shown in 1837 when its ambassadors first reached the shores of England. Every Mormon designated for missionary work by the community is under the latter's absolute orders for two- or four-year periods, during which time he is required to defray his own travelling and sustentation allowances. Such enthusiasm and altruism is infectious. Secondly, Mormons have undoubtedly won many adherents in the United States who were drawn by the saga of Brigham Young's intrepid trek across the Rockies until he reached Salt Lake and there made the desert blossom like the rose. To this day the Mormon State of Utah has a nation-wide reputation for its excellence in the fields of public education, health and social services, and its citizens are justly renowned for their industry, sobriety, frugality, honesty and cheerfulness.[1] Thirdly, the Mormon Creed is extremely simple and those who embrace it are assured of the support of their fellow 'Saints'.

I

The history of Mormonism is the key to unlock its beliefs. Its founder was Joseph Smith, and its greatest organizer was Brigham Young. Smith was born of notorious parents in Sharon, Vermont, New England, late in 1805. From them he inherited credulity and a weak constitution, further enfeebled by epilepsy. His education as his discipline was sadly neglected. Indeed, he openly described himself as 'a rough stone, desiring the learning of heaven alone'. At the age of fifteen, he claimed to have seen a vision and received a call to become a 'prophet of the Most High God'. In 1822 he further claimed to have received an angelic messenger who came directly from the Divine Presence. The burden of the message was that he would find a precious religious volume hidden in a hill. He was informed that this volume was written on plates of gold and contained the history of the former inhabitants of the North American Continent and the fullest account of the Gospel as delivered by Christ to the ancient inhabitants. He would be able to interpret this volume with the aid of two crystals, which were the emblems and the instruments of seers and prophets of former ages.

Four years later he claimed that the angel instructed him where to look for the golden volume and that he immediately dug it up. These golden pages were inscribed, he maintained, in fine hieroglyphics which the Mormons have since identified as 'Reformed Egyptian' script. With the aid of the promised crystals, he claimed that he was enabled to translate the hieroglyphics at sight. Our mystification at the linguistic expertness of this illiterate man is increased by the assurance of egyptologists that Egyptian hieroglyphics remained unchanged

[1] *Vide* John Gunther, *Inside U.S.A.* (Hamish Hamilton, 1947), p. 195.

from the fifth century B.C. until the fourth century A.D. Furthermore, not only is 'Reformed Egyptian' unknown to the egyptologists, but these experts themselves were unable to decipher Egyptian inscriptions until the discovery of the Rosetta stone. We are left to judge between a gigantic fraud and a great miracle, as the explanation of these events.

The English translation of the hieroglyphics, dictated behind a curtain, to scribes, became what is known as the *Book of Mormon*. It was begun at Manchester in 1827 and finished at Fayette, New York State, in 1829. The original manuscript was lost, and only Cowdrey's copy remains. What is much more inconvenient for the enquirer is the disappearance of the original gold volume.

A summary of the contents of the *Book of Mormon* is best given in Smith's words:

'We are informed by these records that America in ancient times has been inhabited by two distinct races of people. The first were called Jaredites, and came directly from the Tower of Babel. The second race came directly from the city of Jerusalem about six hundred years before Christ. They were principally Israelites, of the descendants of Joseph. The Jaredites were destroyed about the time that the Israelites came from Jerusalem, who succeeded them in the inhabitance of the country. The principal nation of the second race fell in battle towards the end of the fourth century. The remnant are the *Indians* who now inhabit the country. This book also tells us that Our Saviour also made His appearance upon this continent after His resurrection: that He planted the gospel here in all its fulness and richness, and power and blessing; that they had apostles, prophets, pastors, teachers, evangelists; the same order, the same priesthood, the same ordinances, gifts, powers and blessing as was enjoyed on the Eastern Continent; that the people were cut off in consequence of their transgressions; that the last of their prophets who existed among them was commanded to write an abridgement of their prophecies, history, etc., and to hide it up in the earth, and that it should come forth and be united with the Bible for the accomplishment of the purpose of God in the last days.'[2]

Thus, Smith's claims as a prophet rest upon a questionable ethnology and dubious history, not to mention that the *Book of Mormon* is to be regarded as a supplement to the Bible and of equal authority.

From being a passive translator, Smith developed into a prophet and legislator with the publication of the *Book of Commandments*, followed by the *Book of Doctrine and Covenants*. These combined an insistence upon the imminence of the Second Advent, with a request to revive the 'charismatic signs' of the primitive Church, including miracles, the gift of tongues, faith-healing, prophecies and continued revelations.

This new religious community became increasingly unpopular, due to its advocacy of polygamy. In consequence, the Mormons were repeatedly obliged to move westwards. The new kingdom of the elect, their 'Zion', was to be Missouri. Thence, after further strenuous objections on the part of their new neighbours, they moved to the vicinity of Commerce in the State of Illinois, where they founded the town of Nauvoo. Here they had to face further persecution and Smith and his brother were incarcerated in Carthage jail at the request of the Governor. On June 27th, 1844, a mob with blackened faces broke into the prison and shot both the brothers. The effect of this murder was to translate Joseph Smith from a mediocrity with an extravagant imagination into a martyr in the minds of his followers.

The prophet's mantle fell upon Brigham Young. In 1847 he started for the Rocky Mountains with a selected group of stalwarts. After overcoming Herculean difficulties, they reached the Great Salt Lake and began, with typical industry, to plough up the infertile land and to plant crops on the

---

[2] Smith's article is printed in I. D. Rupp, *An Original History of the Denominations of the United States* (1844), p. 4.

very spring day of their arrival. In the same autumn 700 wagons arrived at Salt Lake and a year later they were joined by a further thousand wagons. They built a great city and a State of their own as an abiding monument to their faith and industry. Utah was admitted to the comity of the United States in 1895.

II

At first glance, the Mormon creed is that of a simple, evangelical type of Christianity, consisting of three principles: first, faith in God and in Jesus Christ; second, repentance from all sin; and third, baptism for the remission of sin as a preparation for the gift of the Holy Ghost, which is bestowed by the laying-on of hands. Its departure from the norm of historic Christianity can be found in its doctrine of progressive revelations and in the contents of such additional revelations.

The two additions are known as 'baptism for the dead' and 'celestial marriage'. The former is a vicarious Baptism undertaken by living Mormons for their dead ancestors who would otherwise miss the joys of heaven. This custom has been acutely described as 'a retro-active application of the Roman Catholic doctrine of purgatory'.[3]

Apart from ordinary marriage vows which last until death, the Mormons allow 'celestial marriage' which is binding beyond death, for they believe that a man will retain all his earthly wives in heaven and beget children there. The custom of 'celestial marriage' may well be a residual part of their former approval of polygamy. Brigham Young certainly both taught and practised polygamy. A conservative estimate is that he married seventeen wives and had forty-seven children by them. He justified the practice on the authority of the example of the patriarchs of the Old Testament and on the need of a large population to exploit the wildernesses of Utah. The official defence of the practice was that it enabled a godly

[3] 'Saints, Latter Day'—Article by I. W. Riley in Hastings, E.R.E., Vol. XI.

man to multiply the creation of a redeemed humanity more rapidly than monogamy would allow. Polygamy is not officially practised to-day. In fact, Utah was only admitted into the number of the United States in 1895 after its representatives had promised to proscribe polygamy. Some of the cruelty of polygamy was softened by the necessity laid upon every polygamist to obtain both the consent of his previous wife or wives and the sanction of the community, which was dependent upon his economic sufficiency. None the less, it was a custom more suitable to the Old than the New Dispensation. Moreover, even the modified form of polygamy, the 'celestial marriage', contravenes the declaration of our Lord that in heaven there is neither marriage nor giving in marriage.

It was observed earlier that the first principles of Mormonism are apparently thoroughly evangelical. In fact, however, there are serious departures from orthodox Christian teaching on the nature of God and the person and work of Christ. God is conceived of by them as an exalted man. Furthermore, the Mormon priesthood is declared to be itself the Kingdom of God, and to disobey them is to disobey God.

Not only is the unique authority of Jesus as 'The-Word-made-flesh' denied, but the Gospel records are either contradicted or unwarrantably augmented. He is declared to be 'the son of Adam-God and Mary'. Jesus is further said to have married the Marys and Martha at Cana, thus providing a convenient sanction for Mormon polygamy. Irreverent fantasy can proceed no further than the Mormon assertion that Jesus traced His Davidic descent through David's plural wife Bathsheba, and the unwarrantable conclusion that if David had not been a polygamist, there would have been no Messiah. Furthermore, the Atonement wrought by Christ is limited to the pre-Mormon dispensation. Finally, their complete dissociation from the charitable spirit of our Lord is seen in their categorical declaration that all who are not Latter-Day Saints will be everlastingly damned.

III

Admirable as are many of the ethical qualities of the Mormons and the proselytizing zeal of their 2,000 missionaries, their doctrine must be castigated as perversions of 'the faith once delivered to the saints'.

Their faith is not Christo-centric, for Christ is to them merely a fore-runner of Joseph Smith and they have dared even to falsify the Gospel records in order to make the Messiah fit in with their preconceptions. A faith cannot be called 'Christian' with any justice, if it judges the Christ instead of submitting itself to His authority, and if it replaces the 'obedience of faith' by obedience to the dictates of the Mormon hierarchy as the condition of salvation.

The Mormon theory of progressive revelations destroys the finality and the uniqueness of the revelation brought by the incarnate, crucified and risen Lord of history. Indeed, it stands self-condemned by its own mutability. An outstanding example of such convenient divergence is seen in the supersession of the monogamous *Book of Commandments* by the polygamous *Book of Doctrine and Covenants*. The change was dictated, we may surmise, not by a fuller illumination of the Holy Spirit, but by an access of the impulse towards sensuality.

By Old Testament standards (though not by the criteria of the eighth-century prophets), the morality of the Mormons is admirable, but it comes far short of the sacrificial love inculcated in the New Testament. It is a negative, legalistic, even puritanical code. Apart from the unworthy and degrading view of women which polygamy and 'celestial marriage' countenance, it is impossible to forget the utter ruthlessness with which Brigham Young and his 400 'Wolf Hunters' punished the men and women who tried to escape from Salt Lake City in their disillusionment. To prevent such escapes he and his henchmen did not stop at the murder of men, women and children. Furthermore, the autocratic exercise of power by the Mormon hierarchy over the ordinary members is a denial of the liberty of the Christian man and conflicts with our Lord's request to His disciples that they should not exercise authority as the rulers of the Gentiles do, but with the affection of friendship.

Finally, historical criticism and a scrutiny of the spiritual qualifications of the pretended Mormon prophets render their claims improbable in the extreme. The *Book of Mormon* is a palpable forgery, an anthology of quotations from many sources chronologically later than the supposed date of the volume. Nephi, who purports to be a pre-Christian prophet, uses verbatim quotations from the seventeenth-century Westminster *Confession of Faith*. Elsewhere, the book has word-for-word citations from the Authorized Version translation of the Scriptures into English, an excerpt from a Methodist book of discipline, and a quotation from Shakespeare. It is as full of anachronisms as a sponge is of holes.

Furthermore, neither the character of Smith nor of Young lends credibility to their claims to be prophets. Smith was a bank-note forger and it is improbable that this shifty, illiterate and credulous person would have been remembered but for the murder which made him a martyr. Brigham Young shared his predecessor's sensuality, to which he added his own refinements of cruelty. Neither man had the integrity nor the humility which commonly distinguish the prophets of the living God.

VIII

BRITISH-ISRAEL

. . . the Gentiles are fellow-heirs, and fellow-members of the body, and fellow-partakers of the promise in Jesus Christ through the gospel. (Eph. 3.6)

I perceive God is no respecter of persons.
(Acts 10.34)

There is neither Jew nor Greek. . . . Ye are all one man in Christ Jesus. And if ye are Christ's, then ye are Abraham's seed, heirs according to the promise. (Gal. 3.28-9)

BRITISH-ISRAEL is a theory, rather than a sect or heresy, held by some two million adherents within the Protestant Communions. British-Israelites hold that the British Commonwealth of Nations and the United States of America are the descendants of the ten lost tribes of Israel and that they inherit to-day the political promises made by God to ancient Israel. This theory, like many of the tenets of the sects, is based upon highly fanciful exegesis of the Bible.

Protestants have been rightly termed ' the People of a Book '. This was expressed most cogently by Chillingworth when he claimed: 'The Bible and the Bible alone is the religion of Protestants.' To-day it would be desirable to amend this definition to indicate that the Bible was the *basis* of the religion of Protestants. When Martin Luther dared to criticize the corruptions of the later medieval Church in the West, his only authority was 'The Word of God'. This alone, he claimed, was an authority higher than the Church. He therefore demanded a 'Reformation according to the Word of God'. Protestants stand proudly within this great tradition and are thus obliged to measure all policies by 'the rule of faith' in the Holy Scriptures. Our faith, our ethics, our liturgy, are inescapably Biblical.

If the Bible is, in fact, the sole doctrinal authority of Protestants, why are there so many sects amongst Protestants? Here the term 'sects' is to be distinguished from 'denominations' because the latter accept the Scriptures as the supreme rule of faith and life, and differ radically only in their various forms of ecclesiastical government. By the 'sects' is intended the congeries of bodies which have seceded or broken away from the historic Christian Churches to establish their own organizations in opposition. Among a vast and variegated array which includes the Seventh-Day Adventists, Jehovah's Witnesses, Mormons and Russelites, the 'sects' witness to the danger of Biblical exegesis uninfluenced by the traditional wisdom and experience of the Church of the centuries. When once the Bible was issued to the people translated into their native tongues, without assistance in its interpretation, they misunderstood parts of it, ignored other sections of it, and often read into it their presuppositions or prejudices. The anthology of the Bible thus compiled by subjectivism was erected into a variety of religious systems for which the authority of the Biblical record was claimed.

Such, then, was the peril of private and idiosyncratic interpretation of the Scriptures. Equally hazardous was the exclusively literal exegesis of the Scriptures. Unfortunately, this danger does not only beset those outside the historic Christian Churches; it is often found within them. An instance of ingenious private interpretation, literalist in type, may be given here. Sir James Young Simpson, the distinguished Scottish surgeon, was once thwarted in his attempts to introduce chloroform into gynaecology by a group of 'fundamentalist' ministers of religion, who urged the authority of the Creation text, 'In sorrow and labour shalt thou bring forth

thy children'. His retort out-literalized the literalists, by
claiming that he had divine authority in the same narrative
for the use of anaesthetics, for God had put Adam 'into a
deep sleep' before removing his rib. This apparent digression
is relevant to the study of British-Israel, for this is a theory
based upon private and often crassly literalist misinterpreta-
tions of the Bible.

I

The claims of British-Israelitism must now be considered
The necessary information on the principles of the British
Israel World Federation may be found in two of their authori
tative compilations. One is a pamphlet by Commander Studd,
entitled *Britain's Place in Prophecy*, and the other, *The Heri-
tage of the Anglo-Saxon Race*, by M. H. Gaylor, O.B.E.

From a perusal of these expositions, it appears that British-
Israelites hold three basic beliefs. Firstly, they maintain that
the Old Testament prophecies made by God to Abraham and
confirmed to his descendants must be literally and materially
fulfilled. In the second place, they hold that these promises
and subsequent prophecies require for their fulfilment a belief
that the ten tribes of the northern kingdom of Israel must have
persisted as a nation, ruled by a king of the Davidic dynasty.
Thirdly, they claim that Britain, the British Empire, and the
United States of America, are the inheritors of the promises
of God because they are the descendants of the ten lost tribes
of Israel, and because Britain is ruled by a monarch of the
Davidic line.

The last hypothesis they attempt to establish in an ingenious,
if unconvincing, manner. The ten tribes, they maintain, were
taken captive by the Assyrians in the eighth century B.C.
From captivity they wandered over Europe as the Scythians,
Cimmerians, and Goths. From Europe they invaded England
as the Angles, Saxons, Jutes and Normans, commingling their
blood with that of the Ancient Britons. Therefore, they insist,

the citizens of Britain, the British Commonwealth and the Americans, are the inheritors of the divine promises to Abraham and constitute the New Israel, the master-nation. A summary of this fanciful reconstruction of ethnology is provided by one of their own writers:

'Getae, Massagetae, Sacae, Scythians, Goths, Ostro-Goths, Dacians, Khumri, Milesians, Danes, Jutes, Angles, Saxons, Normans—with many another name that could be added —all at last, either by trade or simple migration, but mostly by fierce fighting and conquest the one or the other found their way into these "Isles of the West". They were "sifted among the nations", as God said they would be, but not a "grain" has been lost, and out of them all have truly evolved the English, Scotch, Irish, Welsh of the British Empire, and the American of the United States.'[1]

If their ethnology is fanciful, their philology is fantastic!

The foundation-stone of the entire edifice of British-Israel is the belief that the promises and prophecies of the Old Testament must be fulfilled literally. Otherwise, it is suggested, God is made to appear a liar and a breaker of His Word. One important point, however, seems to be ignored. That is, that nowhere in His Word does God declare that His promises are to be fulfilled to the letter. It is, in fact, quite impossible to discover a literal meaning in much of the Scriptures. Why, therefore, should the promises be interpreted literally and not metaphorically? Scripture has not always a simple, straightforward meaning, any more than everyday speech has.

One instance of the folly of interpreting common parlance literally may be given, for in this respect God's parlance (the Word of God) is analogous. Let us suppose that a young man has recently become engaged, and that his ecstasy finds expression in a love-letter by a quotation from a lyric. He writes to his fiancée that 'My love is like a red, red rose'. He does not imply by this description that she is a ruddy-

[1] L. Sapsworth. The Bible Arch of British-Israel Truth, p. 94.

cheeked country lass with a florid complexion. Nor is this a
subtle way of declaring that she is lovely, but her loveliness
will fade and wither with the years. Least of all does he mean
that her apparently sweet disposition has unsuspected cruelty
lurking beneath it, as thorns below the rose. His meaning
(or rather *one* of the layers of meaning) is that as the rose
is lovely, so is she. The meaning is metaphorical not literal.

The Bible frequently used this metaphorical, short-hand
type of speech—these implicit similes. For instance, our Lord
says, ' I am the light of the world '. This cannot mean that He
is the sun, but that His Person and Message bring illumination to the souls of men darkened by sin. When He says,
' I am the door ', it cannot be interpreted as meaning that
the composition of His body is wood. His meaning is that, as
a door gives entry to a house, so does he open the Kingdom
of Heaven to all believers.

The same test should be applied to the promises of God to
Abraham and his seed. One example of over-facile British-
Israelite exegesis may be considered. God made the following
promise to Jacob: ' I will multiply thy seed as the sand which
is upon the sea-shore.' The following is Commander Studd's
interpretation of this passage:

' They were to be numerous as sand of the sea, suggesting
at least a great sea-faring nation.'[2]

Does the text suggest that Israel shall be a sea-faring nation?
There is not a hint of it. In addition, it seems that Israel had
no trace of sea-fever in its history, for when Solomon built a
port to the north of the Gulf of Akaba for his joint mercantile
enterprises with Hiram, the Phoenician ruler, his fleet had to
be manned with Tyrian sailors. The text simply asserts that
Jacob's descendants shall be as numerous as the grains of sand
upon the sea-shore. The prophetic ' hint ' of a sea-faring
nation originates in the noble Commander's fertile brain, not
in the Bible. We might suggest that the Commander is view-

[2] *Britain's Place in Prophecy*, p. 6.

ing the Scriptures through the telescope of the Royal Navy; it is even possible that like Nelson, he puts a blind eye to the telescope! This is but one opposite example of exegesis that fails by literalizing a metaphor.

Two other texts which are used for 'sanctified imperialism' of the British variety are Jeremiah 25.22, 'the isle beyond the sea', which is interpreted as meaning Britain; and it is said that the promise made to Abraham in Genesis 22.17, 'Thy seed shall possess the gate of his enemies', refers particularly to the British possessions of Gibraltar, Malta, Cyprus and Suez! In fact the literal meaning of the word translated as 'isle' in the former citation is, as the marginal reading in the Revised Version indicates, 'coastland', and the word translated as 'gates' in the latter citation is simply 'cities'. Clearly, this is exegetical ignorance masquerading as originality.

Such fanciful exegesis must be censured, but it does not dispose of the larger questions: How were the promises to Abraham and his seed fulfilled? The New Testament, nevertheless, does dispose of this question in several places. It claims that the promises and prophecies made by God to the chosen people are fulfilled in Jesus Christ and His Community, the New Israel. St. Paul, for example, declares: 'The Gentiles are fellow-heirs and fellow-members of the body, and fellow-partakers of the promise in Christ Jesus through the Gospel'. Elsewhere, referring to our Lord, St. Paul writes, 'In Him are all the promises of God'. In yet another place he states categorically, 'And if ye are Christ's, then are ye Abraham's seed, heirs according to the promise'.

St. Peter may also be summoned as a witness to the truth that the promises of God to Abraham are fulfilled in the Christian Church. He says, in a sermon preached to the Jews but with an eye on the Gentiles, 'Ye are the children of the prophets, and of the covenant which God made with our fathers, saying unto Abraham, And in thy seed shall all the nations of the world be blessed. Unto you *first* God, having raised up Christ Jesus sent Him to bless you, in turning every one of

you away from his iniquities '. Clearly it is the Church which
inherited the fulfilment of the promises in Christ. The
Church had comparatively few converts from Judaism, but
many Gentiles within its fold. The fulfilment of the promises
was not biologically conceived, as the British-Israelites claim
it ought to have been. It was a spiritual fulfilment. Since
the majority of the chosen people rejected Jesus the Messiah,
they had forfeited the promises.

Because these promises were spiritually fulfilled in Christ
and conveyed to His faithful followers, regardless of nationality or race, it is unnecessary to look for any biological fulfilment. This being the case, the second and third principles
of British-Israel are ruled out of court. Since the promises
were spiritually fulfilled and are available for all Christians,
it is superfluous to search for evidence of the history of the
lost ten tribes of Israel. Because the fulfilment of Abraham's
promises has taken place in the Kingdom of God over which
Christ rules as King of kings and Lord of lords, we need not
look to the future for the realization of the divine promises
to Abraham.

II

If the Biblical interpretation of the British-Israelites is
eccentric and their re-writing of history chimerical, how can
their appeal be accounted for? Several factors play an important part in the attraction of British-Israel. First, it appeals
to patriotic people, who find a Biblical warrant for the importance of their nation in the affairs of the world. One might go
further and say that it is peculiarly attractive to those who
believe themselves to be the *Herrenvolk*.

Secondly, it appeals to persons perplexed by the maze of
history, who are searching for a philosophy of history which
will counteract the apparent insignificance of individuals on
the modern scene. To such the Bible offers a key to world-
history.

In the third place, they are unconsciously seeking for an adequate doctrine of the Church as the New Israel of God, believing that God calls peoples, not merely individual units, into His service.

This three-fold appeal is a solemn warning for the Churches. They must be more careful to instruct their charges that the international and interracial Church of Christ has claims that override even patriotism. The Churches must learn from the idiosyncratic exegesis of the British-Israelites the need for sounder Biblical instruction. It seems, in Professor J. R. Coates's phrase, that many within the Churches look upon the Word of God ' as a sort of Bradshaw's Time-table in cypher '.[3] Christians are particularly ignorant of the philosophy of the apocalyptic books of the Bible, which are such a happy hunting-ground for sectarians and schismatics.

III

A detailed critique of British-Israel must now be offered. Our first criticism is that, since New Testament days, the need for an elect nation has disappeared, for it has been met by the international Church of Christ. The final Word of God in the New Testament is that racial distinctions are irrelevant in the matter of salvation. There is no suggestion in it that there can be a master-race. Christ's great mission to the world will be fulfilled by individuals nurtured in community who will gather up other individuals to whom they have proclaimed the Gospel into communities. Such individuals and communities created and confirmed by the Gospel, whatever the race or races included in their membership, are Christ's chosen people, the Church.

Christ is Messiah of all nations alike, and as all nations may be chosen, there is no need for a particular chosen nation. In the redeemed community or race all distinction of nationality, class, race, sex and culture are transcended, for ' there is

[3] Article, *Expository Times*, Vol. LIV, p. 315.

neither Jew nor Greek, circumcision nor uncircumcision, Barbarian, Scythian, bond nor free: but Christ is all in all'. The renascence of doctrines of a privileged race have proved in recent times dangerous to the peace of the nations, and a poison in the veins of the Body of Christ, the Church. Such teaching, it cannot be too often insisted upon, is a flat denial of the Gospel doctrine. It disregards the words of John the Baptist, 'begin not to say within yourselves, We have Abraham to our father'. It refuses to consider seriously St. Paul's saying, 'he is not a Jew which is one outwardly'. It contradicts outright the solemn declaration of our Lord Himself, 'the flesh profiteth nothing'.

It could also be pointed out that the British-Israelites entirely misunderstand the nature of 'election' even in the Old Covenant, for God chose the Israelites for service not for privilege. This was the bitter reminder of the prophecy of Amos, 'You only have I known of all the families of the earth: therefore I will visit upon you all your iniquities'. In the deepest thought of the Old Testament the doctrine of election was expanded in its charity to include universalism: 'Are ye not as the children of the Ethiopians unto me, O children of Israel? saith the Lord. Have not I brought up Israel out of the land of Egypt, and the Philistines from Caphtor, and the Syrians from Kir?' The British-Israelites are anachronisms.

In the second place, they must be accused of imperfectly understanding the nature and authority of the Bible, as their faulty exegesis proves. Whether they deal with the Law, the Prophets, the Writings, the Gospels or the Epistles, they place them on the same level as instructors in Christian doctrine. The Old Testament is more important to them than the New, with the exception of the Book of Revelation. The inspiration of the Bible is not all on the same level: the Bible itself is, in Luther's phrase, the 'cradle of Christ' and the Old Testament must be judged by the Revelation of the Word of God Incarnate, the mind of Christ.

They must be censured for regarding the prophets as prediction-experts. The prophets did not come among the people to foretell distant events; they were there to foretell God's will for their own generation. This distinction is admirably made by Professor J. E. McFadyen in *The Bible and Modern Thought*:

> 'No one who reads such a book as Amos could carry away the impression that its importance lay in prediction. Running through it, doubtless, is the broad announcement that national sin will issue in national ruin, but the value of this lies in its moral interpretation of history, not in its miraculously predictive quality.'

Furthermore, British-Israelite exegesis unwarrantably distinguishes between the fulfilment of passages referring to Israel and those referring to Judah. We may well ask: why should the divine promises made to the whole people apply only to the relatively small segment of the nation which was carried into captivity?

In the third place, the whole import and emphasis of British-Israel leads to a false sense of racial security, to a dangerous racial pride and an unworthy conception of God. Of this implication of their teaching, Dr. James Black has said:

> 'British-Israel theory . . . is dangerously like some modern theories of race superiority which have only brought sorrow, shame and insolence into men's hearts. Quite seriously, I regard this type of idea as one of the dangers to human peace and sanity.'[4]

Fourthly and finally, it must be stated that the subsidiary historical, ethnological and philological arguments used by the champions of British-Israel are contrary to the ascertained facts and are often fantastically improbable. No reputable archaeologist would be found to agree that the Scythians were of Semitic origin as there are no traces of Semitic influence on either their language or their customs. The ethnological link

[4] *New Forms of the Old Faith* (Nelson, 1948), p. 282.

in the British-Israelite historical chain is so weak that Israel's most distinctive customs—circumcision, seventh-day observance, ritual cleanness—have not survived amongst the Scythians, Cimmerians, Angles, Saxons or Celts. We are informed that the languages of the United Kingdom contain many words akin to Hebrew. Thus 'Britain' derives from B'RITH (covenant); 'Tara' from TORAH (law); 'Cymri' from OMRI (king of Israel); while 'Scot' comes from SCYTHIAN, and 'Saxon' is just ISAAC's SON. A glance at the *Concise Oxford Dictionary* would explode these delightful philological balloons. For example, the origin of 'Cymri' is the Old Celtic *Combroges* (compatriots). Each of their other derivations is as arbitrary as this. Expert philologists assure us that there are no possible links in vocabulary, grammar or syntax between the Semitic language of the ten tribes and the Low or High German of the Teutons.

The crux of the whole theory is historical. But many other claims for the lost ten tribes have been made. The Mormons urge that the Indians of North America are they, while other peoples that have been suggested for the same rôle are the Laplanders and the Mexicans. The Joint Editor of Valentine's *Jewish Encyclopedia* maintains that there are only two claims for descent from the lost tribes which have any serious basis, namely those of the Afghans and the Nestorians.

IV

It would be unsatisfactory to let the matter end there. With the British-Israelites we must also recognize that God fulfils His purpose through nations as well as through individuals, though it is the individuals which determine the character of a nation. God's judgments are made known in the arena of history. Nations, as well as individuals, may be the instruments of the divine justice punishing aggressors. The Old Testament indicates that God may anoint nations other than His chosen people Israel, to be the instruments of judgment on His chosen but impenitent people. For this reason Elijah could speak of Hazael, whom he anointed as king of Syria, as God's agent; similarly, but in more direct fashion, Isaiah could speak of the king of Persia, as seen by God, in the following words: 'Thus saith the Lord to his anointed, to Cyrus . . . I will gird thee though thou hast not known me.' The same prophet says, 'O Assyrian, the rod of my anger . . .' implying that God's will is made effectual through other nations of the world. Similarly, the dark signature of divine displeasure is written over the ruined cities of Europe. But the nations whom God selects to fulfil His purposes are never master-races; they are servant-races—they exist in order to obey the behests of the Almighty. It is an election to responsibility and even to suffering, as Israel knew of old. No nation is elected by God to lord it over other peoples, as a *Herrenvolk* or imperial regime.

In this strictly limited sense, when to suffer oppression would be worse than to draw the bloody sword of justice, nations may be the agents of divine justice, though never as self-appointed agents. Nations as well as individuals can fall a prey to hypocrisy and Pharisaism. In this sense also, nations that inherit the traditions of a Christian civilization—the so-called 'Christian countries'—are under obligation to protect and perpetuate the Christian faith, and are thus elected.

But the Bible speaks of another sword, more effectual than the sword of justice; it is the Sword of the Spirit, the Word of God. This alone will provide the basis for communal and international integration. Justice is founded upon the threat of coercion, but the Sword of the Spirit is love. Men can be cowed into terror by the sword of justice or war, and when men and nations neglect or spurn the rights of individuals and of other nations, the last recourse of the defenders of divine justice may be this ugly weapon of fear. But lasting unity among the nations becomes possible only when men see the love of God in the Cross of Christ stooping to conquer, embracing man in his loathsomeness and setting him on his feet again. Such divine reconciliation is the only enduring basis of international comity.

The Christian's task is therefore to vanquish the rebellious hearts of men by the weakest thing in the world—the wounds of a crucified King. But the weakness of God is stronger than the power of men, as His folly is wiser than the sagacity of men.

IX

MORAL RE-ARMAMENT OR THE OXFORD GROUP

We reckon therefore that a man is justified by faith apart from the works of the law. (Romans 3.28)

THE religious society which owes its origin to the inspiration of Frank D. Buchman has been known by various titles, of which the most popular was 'The Oxford Group' and the most recent is 'Moral Re-armament' (a term coined by the founder to mark a new development of the Movement on his sixtieth birthday in 1938). Other names have been 'The New Groupers' and 'The First Century Christian Fellowship'.

I

As in the case of many new impulses of the religious spirit, the Movement is unintelligible apart from some knowledge of the odyssey of its founder, the Rev. Frank D. Buchman, a minister of the Lutheran Church of the United States. He was born of German-Swiss stock in 1878 in Pennsburg, Pennsylvania. He received the orthodox training for the Lutheran ministry, begun at Muhlenberg College and completed at Mount Airy Seminary. His first charge was the impoverished Lutheran congregation in Overbrook in his native State of Pennsylvania, whither he had deliberately gone because a college friend had accused him of overweening personal ambition. Here he founded a boys' settlement, and later resigned his charge after a disagreement with its trustees.

He then travelled in Italy and England, and, while in the latter country, experienced a radical conversion while listening to a woman speaker at the Keswick evangelical convention, testifying to the transformation the Cross of Christ had wrought in her life. As a consequence he was convinced that his relationships with the trustees in Overbrook must be improved and he wrote to the six with whom he had quarrelled letters of apology. These were headed with the words of Isaac Watts' famous verse:

> ' When I survey the wondrous Cross
>   Where the young Prince of Glory died,
>   My richest gain I count but loss,
>   And pour contempt on all my pride.'

The letters continued:

' MY DEAR FRIEND,
   I have nursed ill-will against you. I am sorry. Forgive me?

Yours sincerely,
FRANK.'[1]

Although these letters were unanswered, Buchman found personal relationships with these gentlemen no longer strained. His next appointment was that of Y.M.C.A. Secretary at the State University of Pennsylvania where his efforts to improve the moral tone of the institution, to which he had been recommended by Dr. John R. Mott, were remarkably successful. During this time he began to develop the principles for which the Oxford Movement has since become famous.

Because he had found peace of mind by submitting his own will to the divine will, he argued that religion was not essentially a matter of the intellect or of the heart, but of the will. He was convinced that his life's work would consist

[1] Speeches of Frank D. Buchman, *Remaking the World* (Blandford, 1946), p. 191.

of persuading others to live by the will of God, through sharing his own experience. The element of the confession of sins and victory over them became paramount in his thoughts at this time, and he summed these up in the sentence: 'The degree of our freedom from sin is the degree of our desire to be free.' The next few years were spent in widespread travelling and working out his religious methodology in greater detail. As he went from nation to nation he became convinced that 'life-changing' was the only remedy for the nationalism which led to wars, and it was this line of thought which was ultimately to lead him to re-christen the Movement as 'Moral Re-armament'.

He was in Asia and in the United States during the First World War and it was in the former continent that the first house-party was held. This took place in Kuling, in China in 1918 at the home of a prominent lawyer and was attended by a hundred guests. The discussion of religion at such informal gatherings in unorthodox settings gave the Movement a sense of novelty and sincerity.

In 1921 he was back again in England and visited the ancient universities at the request of two Anglican bishops. At Cambridge he obtained the services of Harold Begbie as a devoted adherent and a popular propagandist, but he was even more successful in his attempts to evangelize the war-scarred undergraduates at Oxford. Here he developed a second feature of the Movement, namely the 'Quiet Time'. Its purpose, in his own words was

'to give that hour of the day from five to six in the morning when the phones were unlikely to ring to listen for the Still Small Voice to inspire and direct. . . .'[2]

From Oxford the Movement spread to Holland in 1927, and to South Africa in the two succeeding years, where, incidentally, it was first named 'The Oxford Group'.

In the years 1932 to 1934 the Movement made rapid advances

[2] *Remaking the World* (Blandford, 1946), p. 194.

in Canada and in the latter year it was invited to Norway by Mr. C. J. Hambro, the President of the Norwegian Parliament. In 1935 the Oxford Group teams were officially welcomed in Denmark by the Primate of that country. In 1938 they were warmly received in Sweden, while they had been welcomed by Switzerland as early as 1933. In 1946 the headquarters of the Moral Re-armament Movement, with its permanent staff, was established at Caux in Switzerland, and annual assemblies with delegates attending from all over the world are held there.

From Keswick to Caux is a long spiritual journey, but, if Buchman had shed some of his orthodox Christian doctrines, his enthusiasm, strategy, and sincerity had produced a world-wide organization which had received tributes from statesmen and leaders of public opinion in many nations.

II

The chief difficulty in attempting to set forth its teaching, is that this organization seems to remain interdenominational at the cost of freeing itself from any positive doctrinal commitments. It may, therefore, better be considered as a system, a way of life, rather than as a creed. It should also be noted that it repudiates the designation of 'sect', and urges its members to revitalize the Churches to which they belong.

If it can be said to have a doctrinal ethos rather than a platform, then it may be recalled that its founder inherited the traditions of German Lutherans and English Evangelicals. It seems, however, that the pragmatism of the United States, coupled with a desire for improvement of character, is its present distinguishing mark. Unfriendly observers amongst the theologians have dubbed it 'Pelagian'. Certainly, the chief emphasis seems to be on reformation rather than on regeneration, on works rather than on faith, on the response of men rather than on the revelation of God, on sanctification apart from justification.

G

Men and women, especially the young, the well-to-do and the influential, are invited to attend house-parties. There the atmosphere is marked by cordiality and candour. Each new-comer is attached to a Grouper of the same sex. In this happy, informal comradeship members of the Group speak openly of their experience of being changed, omitting no details of the past life which they have now renounced. The guest is encouraged to take his or her part in the activity known as 'sharing'; that is, to confess to another Grouper the sins which have stood between him and God.

This person is then confronted with the 'Four Absolutes'— absolute honesty, purity, unselfishness and truth, the ideals of the Group and the standards by which the success or failure of the individual member is to be judged. The Group claims that 'placing these four points for a Christian life as absolute ones is placing Christ as the absolute example to which by the help of God we can aspire'.[3] The Group further advocates the following religious discipline as the means for attaining the 'Four Absolutes':

'1. The Sharing of our sins and temptations with another Christian life given to God, and to use Sharing as witness to help others, still unchanged, to recognize and acknowledge their sins.

2. Surrender of our life, past, present, and future, into God's keeping and direction.

3. Restitution to all whom we have wronged directly or indirectly.

4. Listening to, accepting, relying on God's Guidance and carrying it out in everything we do or say, great or small.'[4]

In many ways the Oxford Group's system of spiritual discipline is the revival, under a modern nomenclature, of the older techniques of evangelism, with the significant difference that

[3] The Layman with a Notebook, *What is the Oxford Group?* (Oxford Press, 1933), p. 7.
[4] *ibid.*, pp. 8-9.

the Group seeks for individual decisions not for mass commitments. 'Life-changing' corresponds to conversion, 'sharing' to witness, and 'house-parties' to testimony-meetings.

By means of these techniques the Moral Re-armament organization is confident of winning the world for God; and, as nothing succeeds like success, it makes a point in its public meetings and periodicals of listing its 'trophies' in the form of notable persons who have joined its ranks. Its members sum up their *credo* in the following way:

> 'When man listens, God speaks.
> When man obeys, God acts.
> When God acts, nations change.'

Through 'surrendered' lives, Moral Re-armament looks forward to a 'God-controlled world'.

III

Moral Re-armament has undoubtedly many advantages that commend it to the modern world, many of which might be imitated by the historic Churches. It represents, in the first place, a much-needed reaction from the hysteria of mass revivals. The stress is laid on the evangelism of the individual, as proven by a 'changed' life and the acceptance of a spiritual regimen and the duty to witness by 'sharing' his experience. Part of Dr. Buchman's success is undoubtedly due to his flair for describing old techniques in up-to-date terminology. 'Sharing' for example, is often described as a part of 'soul-surgery' or 'spiritual therapeutics'.

Secondly, the Movement has concentrated on winning 'key-persons' to its allegiance. The older revivalism concentrated on the down-and-outs, Moral Re-armament on the 'up-and-outs'. It bases its technique of selection on the correct assumption that the worldly are more impressed by the gaining of famous and significant adherents than by impressive statistics.

The same emphasis also explains why the Movement is frequently criticized for snobbishness.

Thirdly, it has challenged a merely nominal Christianity by its enthusiasm and its double demand: for surrendered lives and the need for witnessing to others. Conventional Christians have usually been tongue-tied or they have left the duty of gaining converts to the professionals, the ministers and clergy.

Fourthly, it has selected terminology which is simple and intelligible, whereas historic Christianity has rarely expounded its doctrines in terms that are understood by the wayfaring man. It may also be, of course, that the organization has over-simplified its terminology and omitted some of the distinctive features of the Christian life and teaching.

Fifthly, in place of the older orthodoxy which emphasized the importance of a correct doctrinal statement (whether in creed or confession), Moral Re-armament insists on the importance of changed lives. This represents a welcome return to our Lord's advice: ' By their fruits shall ye know them.' At the same time, however, life without doctrine is as futile as doctrine without life. Ethical fruits presupposes theological roots, and justification is the pre-requisite for sanctification.

Sixthly, Moral Re-armament has discovered valuable new methods of evangelical strategy in its house-parties and public meetings for testimony, and, following the example of the mediaeval and modern Church, makes use of religious drama.

Finally, the newcomer is bound to be impressed by the *camaraderie* of the Oxford Group. As contrasted with the lack of any Christian family life in many churches, the Group is a living fellowship of equals meeting, as friends should, in each other's homes and throughout the week. In their case ' See how these Christians love one another' is not a sarcasm, but a testimonial.

IV

The weaknesses of the Movement outweigh the advantages which have been mentioned. The first deficiency of the Groupers is their subjectivity. They believe that theology is entirely a construct of individual experience, whereas in fact theology is partly determinative of our experience; for we respond to the revelation of God recorded in the Scriptures and confirmed by the Holy Spirit in the experience of the Churches. To overestimate human experiences in comparison with the mighty acts of God is commonly a fault of the intuitive, mystical approach to God.

Secondly, as might be expected from the foregoing, the Oxford Group displays a lamentable ignorance of Christian doctrine. This was the criticism of twelve Anglican clergymen in Oxford who watched the Group in its hey-day there:

'In our opinion they dangerously overemphasize the importance of subjective experience in spiritual things; with the result that in their public meetings, as also in their private testimonies, little is heard about the objective facts of the Gospel of the work of Christ for us.'[5]

Their neglect of theology leads to such absurdities as the following incident. The present writer once attended a meeting at their London headquarters in Hays Mews where one leading Grouper claimed that the most impressive event of his life took place at a Group meeting in India where Hindus, Buddhists and Moslems all recited the Lord's Prayer together. The futility of such an assertion lies in the fact that the Buddhist does not believe in God, the Hindu thinks of an impersonal Principle, and the Moslem has a notion of the Deity as a wily but all-powerful oriental potentate! Happily, however, the nature of God is not altered by our unworthy conceptions of Him.

[5] Letter in *The Guardian*, issue of June 24th, 1932.

Thirdly, Groupers seem to judge Christianity purely by the pragmatic test; that is, by results alone. It is extremely doubtful whether their experiences of 'life-changing' are Christocentric. The improved lives are more often self-improvement and are the results of reformation more often than regeneration.

Fourthly, many writers have criticized the custom of public 'sharing', or confession of sins. Both Rom Landau and Beverley Nichols, who gave the Movement most sympathetic consideration, and were for a time members of it, insist that Groupers aggrandize and exaggerate their sins in order to make their conversions appear more dramatic.

Fifthly, their method of seeking the guidance of God has been severely criticized. Bishop Chavasse has written of this:

> 'And how can people who are so woefully and wilfully ignorant of doctrine, as the average Grouper is, rightly discriminate which is from God and which is not from God?'[6]

Thoughts generated in a vacuum have no validity for those who wish to be guided by the only standard for Christians, the mind and example of Christ. Moreover, some of the suggestions received in the relaxed state are often trivial and sometimes even ludicrous. Furthermore, the Oxford Group's laudable insistence upon obeying the will of God, ignores the fact that the intellectual and emotional life of man is also renewed by grace.

Sixthly, there is a meretricious superficiality about much Moral Re-armament teaching. Dr. Buchman's mnemonics are jejune and often seriously disloyal to the Biblical witness. PRAY, he says, means 'Powerful Radiograms Always Yours'. This ignores the whole element of petitionary prayer which is more analogous to a transmitter than to a radiogram. JESUS, he declares, means 'Just Exactly Suits Us Sinners'. In

[6] C. M. Chavasse and others, *The Oxford Group Movement: Some Evaluations*, p. 10.

fact, the name means that ' He shall save the people from their sins '.

Seventhly, the Oxford Group cannot be entirely freed from the charge of snobbery, social and spiritual. Their predilection for the company of the famous and the affluent, in preference to that of the ordinary, is well known. Moreover, their attitude to the ordinary churchgoer frequently savours of Pharisaism. They need not be so self-consciously the leaven of the lump, for the Master who bade His disciples act as leaven also urged them: ' Let your light so shine before men that they may see your good works and glorify your Father which is in heaven.'

Finally, they must be judged by their own ideal for themselves. Their earliest name for themselves was the 'First Century Christian Fellowship'. This name has been dropped, but not the comprehensive ideal which it enshrined. Their aim is an impossible one, for they cannot start in the twentieth century as though the Holy Spirit had not guided the Church in the intervening centuries in the development of its theology and its liturgy. Of this defect Dr. J. K. van Baalen writes:

' It is a denial of the historic guidance of the Holy Spirit in the name of spontaneous guidance.'[7]

Furthermore, the Oxford Group misrepresents the first century, for apostolic Christians did not form groups to exchange experiences; they founded churches with a tradition of teaching, worship, sacraments, prayer and ecclesiastical government. The great Reformers, Luther, Calvin and Wesley, did not underestimate the place of the Church in the *Acts of the Apostles*.

In conclusion, Moral Re-armament represents ' an unpaid bill of the Churches '. It has, in fact, succeeded where many of the Churches have failed. Protestantism in rejecting the confessional of the Roman Catholic Church has made the mistake of neglecting confession that has content and goes into

[7] *The Chaos of Cults* (Eerdmans, Grand Rapids, Michigan, 1938), p. 175.

detail. It has also frequently forgotten that restitution is the index of sincerity in making a confession. It has been content with a Sunday acquaintance with our fellow-Christians, which is considerably less than the New Testament meant by 'the fellowship of the saints'. It has dangerously left the task of witnessing to the professionals of the Church—to those ordained to preach. The theological language of the Church has to be translated into the vocabulary of the twentieth century. The Oxford Groupers may be regarded as a foe of the Christian Church in their disinterestedness in doctrine; but they are more significantly identified as the gadflies of the Church than as its heretics. The Church has the light: it needs the warmth of the Oxford Group.

X

ASTROLOGY

*It is in Christ that the entire Fulness of Deity has
settled bodily, it is in Him that you reach your full
life, and He is the Head of every angelic Ruler and
Power.* (Col. 2.9-10)

OURS is often proudly described as the 'Scientific Age', yet
the prevalence of popular superstition seems to deny the truth
of the claim. Nor is it only desperately poor, unintelligent
or credulous folk who are superstitious. To take but a single
example—so widespread is the belief that number thirteen
is unlucky, that houses bearing this number are difficult to
let, and even great liners scheduled to leave port on the thir-
teenth day of the month postpone their departure until a few
minutes after midnight. The increase in superstition is undeniably caused by the decrease in a living faith in God.

This is illustrated by an incident in the life of Colonel
T. E. Lawrence of Arabia recounted in *Revolt in the Desert*.
One evening in the desert he offered his field-glasses to a group
of Arab chieftains. They scanned the sky with them. They
talked together of telescopes of even greater power, revealing
more and more stars. One of them said, 'When we see them
all there will be no night in the heavens.' Another, however,
asked, 'Why are the Westerners wanting all? Behind our
few stars we can see God, who is not behind your millions.'

That story is a parable of the pilgrimage of Western man.
As a poet has written, 'The heavens have grown far off and
become astronomical'. Modern Western man has discovered
and named hundreds of new stars, but in the process he has

blotted out the face of God from the heavens. Two groups of people must bear responsibility for this situation, though they do not share culpability equally. The first group comprises the natural scientists who have probed the immediate truths about the constitution of the universe, but have not probed far enough to reach the Ultimate Cause. The second and more culpable group consists of the astrologers who maintain that the stars exercise the profoundest influence on human destiny. For such, the stars and the planets supplant God in the universe.

Lest it should be assumed by the reader that astrology is an outworn and rapidly dying superstition, and that the writer is flogging a dead horse, it must be insisted (with evidence) that the horse is not only alive but vigorously kicking as well. For this assertion the following evidence is offered.

Firstly, the astronomical magazine *Prediction* advertises in its pages no fewer than forty-five astrologers eager to predict the future by means of horoscopes. In addition, five Sunday newspapers in Britain, with a wide circulation, give their astrologers pride of place. Lyndoe writes for *The People*, R. H. Naylor for *The Sunday Express*, Nostradamus II for *The Sunday Dispatch*, Adrienne Arden for *The News of the World*, and Gipsy Petulengro for *The Sunday Chronicle*. In other words, astrology is an essential component of a successful Sunday newspaper. Mr. Ivor Thomas, M.P., in his Oxford World Affairs pamphlet on the Press, computes that *The News of the World* and *The People* are read by half the British population during their time of maximum leisure. To this significant fact should be added another: thousands of people in England purchase copies of *Old Moore's Almanac*. From this it will be realized that astrology, far from being dead, is galloping through the homes of the people of Britain. Its influence varies from person to person. Some watch its progress with cynical amusement; some condemn it outright as superstitious nonsense; but numbers say, 'Perhaps there's something in it'. Thereby the latter group admits that predictions may be more than coincidental.

It is precisely because Christians are custodians of right thinking and the guardians of the conscience of the nation, that they must take serious account of astrology as having a powerful influence on the lives of men and women, and as being a sinister substitute for true religion. The first requirement, therefore, is for a knowledge of astrology and its claims.

I

What, then, is the nature of astrology? It is the belief that the planets and the stars exert a powerful and profound influence on the course of human events, both national and personal. The astrologer claims that by noting the exact positions of the planets and stars at the moment of the individual's birth, he can give valuable information as to that person's character and probable destiny. The astrologer's first claim, then, is that the stars rule the courses of our lives, and his second that he can predict with a fair degree of certainty what that influence will be. He also claims that by studying the horoscope of famous men of affairs he is able to foretell the future of nations as well as of individuals.

II

How, we may ask, did such a curious belief originate? Astrology began as a scientific pursuit in ancient Babylon and was based on a careful observation of the heavens in the dry, cloudless air of its deserts. It was noticed, firstly, that there were, in addition to the fixed stars, several 'wandering' stars (that is the origin of the name 'planets'), and that two of these remained near the sun. These latter are now named Mercury and Venus. Three others, now known as Mars, Jupiter and Saturn, moved less restrictedly. Since the sun, as the source of light and heat of the world, marked the succession of seasons, and the moon the succession of months and weeks and affected the tides, it was assumed that the other planets also influenced human lives. They were all deified or regarded as the abodes of the gods.

Astrologers observed, in the second place, that the planets moved within the confines of a certain path in the sky which passed through a broad band of stars. Since they also noted that the moon when traversing this path occasionally intervened between the earth and the sun, causing an eclipse, they named this path the 'ecliptic'.

Thirdly, the astrologers divided the 'ecliptic' into twelve compartments or 'houses' over each of which there was a presiding deity. These ultimately became the present signs of the Zodiac, one apportioned to each month. Each planet was given two 'houses' and was believed to modify the influence of the presiding deity of the 'house' when within it.

Finally, in the words of Professor Clement Rogers, 'the mapping-out of the planets in their various houses with their fixed stars moving with the Zodiac, and the calculating of their supposed combined influence on a person at the moment of birth was called a horoscope'.[1]

For ancient Babylonians who were polytheists there was nothing absurd in such a view. For the astrologer in the modern world, who rarely believes in a God, and in many gods even less frequently, the idea is fantastic. He is therefore forced to believe that the planets and the stars themselves guide our human destinies. His beliefs have all the quixotry of materialism. For he holds that huge, lifeless masses of volcanic material of different temperatures and sizes control human lives. He expects us to believe that a whirling and semi-liquid stone in outer space plots the course of each separate life. The Babylonians, at least, thought that superhuman beings directed the stars, which in turn guided the lives of individuals. Our present-day astrologers want us to accept something even more preposterous—that stars without gods rule our national and personal destinies.

[1] C. F. Rogers, *Astrology and Prediction* (S.C.M., 1948), p. 30.

III

Detailed evaluations of astrological claims can now be considered. The first charge against astrology is that it contradicts common sense. It is difficult to believe that this universe is so disordered that man is controlled by something less significant than himself in the created order. How foolish it would seem if it were suggested that horses and dogs rule the lives of men! How much more absurd, then, to believe that mobile stones manage men! One has only to imagine the composition of a prayer to the astral deities to realize the inadequacy of astrology as a religion. 'Our Volcanic Fathers who are in the Heavens', it would run, 'your conflicting wills be done on earth as in heaven. . . .' A comparison with the Lord's Prayer would lay bare its pitiable inadequacy as a substitute.

A second criticism would emphasize the contradictions and confusions of the predictions actually made by the astrologers. They almost invariably differ from one another. Where they appear to have made a correct forecast, it is probably because they have been vague and non-committal. One of many instances will be given to demonstrate how events have falsified predictions. Poland was invaded on the 1st September, 1939 and two days later England declared war on Germany. A mere fortnight before these grave events (on the 13th August, 1939), Lyndoe wrote: 'Anyone who listens to and believes that war-by-the-end-of-August rubbish is beyond hope.' Could anyone have discredited himself more completely as a false prophet? On August 29th, 1939, Naylor wrote, 'There will be no war over Dantzig'. He, too, was proved to be in error by the immediate course of events. The considered judgment of Father Bede Frost would be difficult to improve upon. He wrote:

'Their predictions are generally vague and inaccurate— where accurate any well-informed student of affairs could have done the same.'

Their patent differences from one another, their gross in-accuracies, and their customary vagueness, prove that they are radically unsound and unworthy of credibility.

In the third place, the calculations of previous generations of astrologers have been discredited by the discovery of three planets since 1781. In that year Uranus was first discovered by Herschel and it was found to have an equatorial diameter three times that of the earth. In 1845 Neptune was discovered and Pluto as recently as 1930. How, we have a right to demand, could astrologers accurately predict the influence of planets on human affairs when they were unaware of the existence of three of eight already known to exist? Moreover, it is not improbable that further discoveries of stars and planets will further continue to embarrass the astrologers.

Fourthly, the fundamental confusion of astrology was shown almost two thousand years ago by Cicero in his *De Divinitate*. He impaled astrologers on the horns of the following dilemma: If events happen by chance, it is impossible to fore-see them; if events are fated to take place, it is impossible to prevent them.

For these four reasons it is possible to make the blunt assertion that astrology is contrary to common sense. Both scientists and Christians join forces in condemning astrology as quackery and superstitious humbug. The Christian, in-deed, goes much further in his condemnation, for he asserts that astrology is a substitute for and a denial of the Christian faith.

IV

We turn, therefore, to a Christian critique of astrology. A belief in astrology denies the true religious attitude of faith. Our trust, as Christians, is in the Father of our Lord Jesus Christ, the Ruler of the Universe. His beloved Son has taught us to believe that we are under the Fatherly governance of God. Astrologers invite us to transfer our trust in God to them, and to rule our lives in accordance with their predictions.

True wisdom is enshrined in St. Paul's advice to the Galatians
—not to put their trust in the 'beggarly elements'. We cannot ask God to abdicate in favour of the impersonal stars of
outer space. 'The Lord thy God is one God; Him only shalt
thou serve.' The Christian is under a solemn engagement to
obey this commandment. He has no alternative but to place
his trust in God, and God alone. Moreover, his Bible reminds
him of the folly and impotence of the astrologers in the ironic
challenge of the prophet Isaiah: 'Thou art wearied in the
multitude of thy counsels: let now the astrologers, the star-
gazers . . . save thee from the things that shall come upon
thee.'[2]

The Christian quarrels with astrology in the second place
because its tenets are a fundamental denial of the freedom
which is the very context of our spiritual and moral life. We
repudiate astrology with Shakespeare:

> 'Men are at some times masters of their fates:
> The fault, dear Brutus, is not in our stars
> But in ourselves that we are underlings.'

We know that our chief dignity as human beings lies in the
fact that we are made in the image of God, created for willing
co-operation with Him. The astrologers would make puppets
of us, pulled by astral strings. But as Christ's freemen we
cannot return to a beggarly belief in star-gazing and star-
government.

Finally, for the astrologer the future tense is all important.
For the Christian, however, the present must engage his chief
attention, though he has, as it were, a weather-eye on the
future. He recalls that his Master said, 'Be not therefore
anxious for the morrow: for the morrow will be anxious for
itself'. He diagnoses such anxiety as scepticism and unfaith.
In this life we are required to walk along a tortuous path with
guidance sufficient for each day's journey. We are ignorant
of what the future holds in store, apart from the blessed hope

[2] Isa. 47.13.

of life everlasting. It is enough for us to know that the future is in the capable and beneficent hands of God. For that reason we have done with pitiable pryings and petty peep-holes into the future. These are quite unnecessary for those who trust the living God.

V

What steps can be taken to provide a practical cure for astrology? In the first place, a course in elementary astronomy would show that material objects can only have physical results and cannot, therefore, affect the personal characters and destinies of individuals. Secondly, some understanding of psychology would show that the credulity of the devotees of astrology is fed upon the ambiguities of those who make predictions and upon the widespread interest of the general public in successful prognostications and its apathy to the normal and infinitely more frequent failures.

The most effective antidote is, of course, the science of God, theology. A vital belief in the one true God of righteousness and love defeats the polytheism of astrology. Christians know that ' all things work together for good to those who love God, who co-operate with His purpose '. They accept the assurance of Jesus Christ who could say, when His body was mangled on the cross and His mind a tempest of torment, ' Father, into Thy hands I commend My spirit '. The Christian sentry therefore says to the astrologer, ' Advance to be recognized. Surrender your antiquated arms, for you are a foe of the faith.'

XI

OPEN-AIR RELIGION

. . . he left not himself without witness in that he did
good, and gave you from heaven rains and fruitful
seasons, filling your hearts with food and gladness.

(Acts 14.17)

SOME years ago *Punch* satirized the prevalent Pantheism of
our times in a cartoon. It depicted a man, obviously the first
cousin of the Pharisee, who pompously asserted, 'I worship
God in the Cathedral of the Pines, and in the Diocese of
Nature'. This cartoon is evidence of a widespread revolt
from the formal services of the Christian Churches, which
takes the form sometimes of desiring 'communion with
Nature'.

Emile Cammaerts puts the case for 'open-air' worship
as strongly as possible, recollecting his own youthful
romanticism:

'I never missed a Sunday walk and thought that I found in
a wood a stronger inspiration than that which I could find
in a church. The music of birds and waving branches were
better than any organ, and the smell of dead leaves and
pines scorched by the earth better than incense. The trunks
of beeches and the high vaults of their branches were the
columns and arches of my cathedral.'[1]

But the same author, on maturer consideration, admits that

[1] *The Flower of the Grass*, p. 12.

H

his earlier attachment to nature-worship was sentimental and misanthropic in character.

The charge of sentimentalism cannot be substantiated in the best Nature-poetry, as, for instance, in *The Prelude* of William Wordsworth. But even he, according to Aldous Huxley, would not have been a Nature-mystic had he lived in the tropics, instead of in the English Lake District. Sentimentalizing Pantheism is seen typically in a poem by Dorothy Frances Gurney, who writes:

> ' The kiss of the sun for pardon,
> The song of the birds for mirth.
> One is nearer God's heart in a garden
> Than anywhere else on earth.'

The Christian may find in the loveliness of a rose a hint of the Divine Artist; but for the revelation of God's heart he would not go to an English garden, but to the garden of Gethsemane, and for pardon to the cross.

It is to be feared that many who have left the official worship of the Church, ostensibly to worship God in nature, are really devotees of golf, or tennis, or hiking. These ' blue-domers', as the late Archbishop William Temple termed them,[2] are not generally to be found kneeling beneath tree-trunks, rapt in adoration. On the other hand, there are certain spirits who claim in all sincerity that in the grandeur of nature they are moved to worship the Creator. Even if this be true, is it an adequate substitute for the worship of the God and Father of our Lord Jesus Christ? Do such worshippers actually find themselves in contact with the living God, and humbled to repentance before Him? Or, do they merely feel, like Wordsworth, ' a sense sublime', instead of the Supreme God and Redeemer?

The second charge against nature-worship is that it leads to misanthropy, or is the result of such dislike of humanity. Christian worship is essentially the worship of the Body of

[2] *How Christians Worship,* ed. Eric Fenn (S.C.M. Press, 1942), p. 20.

Christ, the redeemed community, not the voluntary association when convenient of like-minded religious enthusiasts. Manifestly, Nature-worship is, by contrast, a refusal to worship God in the way He has ordained, 'in the presence of all His people'.

This is not, of course, to deny that occasionally Christian worship out-of-doors may be permitted. This has been the custom of the Churches when, for instance, the people would not come to the House of God, and the Church has had to go to the people. Franciscan friars and Methodist field-preachers conducted memorable open-air services amongst the uncommitted. Similarly, in the days of persecution Christians perforce worshipped God whenever they could gather in comparative safety. In the third century the faithful worshipped in the catacombs of Rome; in the sixteenth and seventeenth centuries the Nonconformists worshipped in the barns or fields of England. But special circumstances demanded emergency measures. The most convenient place for Christian worship is the church or chapel.

I

For a theological evaluation of nature-worship, we must turn to a sermon preached by the apostle Paul at Lystra. The two apostles, Paul and Barnabas, were mistaken for Greek deities and, to their acute embarrassment, the people prostrated themselves at their feet. St. Paul immediately pointed out that he and Barnabas were men of like passions as themselves, and were unworthy of the veneration of the people. The Living God alone, he declared, deserved to be worshipped. To make this point in a way that the simple heathen could understand, St. Paul requested them to give thanks to the God of nature. This God had obviously done great things which a mere man such as himself could not accomplish: indeed, this true God had sent them the harvest. 'And he left not himself without witness, in that he did good, and gave you from heaven rains and fruitful seasons, filling your hearts with food and gladness.'

It will be observed that the glorifying of God was only the first and most elementary stage in the worship of the true God. It was as if St. Paul had said: 'You must have a worthy object of worship; but you cannot worship Barnabas or myself. Then worship God the Giver who is the Lord of the Harvest.' It was advice given to ignorant men, taking their first halting steps towards God.

Such a religion is only the primary stage in the school of the spirit. It is a worship of the tangible and obvious benefits derived from God the Creator. True and mature worship stands much higher in the scale of spiritual values. St. Bernard of Clairvaux gives an admirable definition of the degrees of love, which can easily be transferred to the degrees of worship, for worship is essentially the expression of our love for God. These degrees are: first, love of self; second, love of God for man's sake; third, love of God for Himself; and finally, love of man and all things for God's sake.

The pagans of Lystra were being invited to the second stage: love of God for man's sake. Spiritually they were mere babes, and had to be fed on milk before they could digest the strong meat of the Gospel. It seems clear that many of the devotees of open-air worship, as also numerous Christians who esteem the Harvest Festival as the outstanding celebration of the Christian Year, are only standing on the second rung of the ladder of worship. This kind of love for God is not dissimilar in quality from the love of the small boy for his favourite aunt, because she sends him postal-orders. The small boy is not really devoted to his aunt; he is devoted to postal-orders. The worshipper of the God of nature or the God of the harvest is in reality a worshipper of the landscape or of his own stomach. His worship is the expression of gratitude, it is true; but such worship is adolescent and immature.

II

Moreover, the worship of the God of nature is beset with difficulties. For this God does not, as his worshippers assume, always appear in a benevolent mood in His creation. Can one offer up a harvest thanksgiving in a desert, or after a drought? Can one thank God for a field full of thistles? One choice spirit, the prophet Habakkuk, could and did. His prophecy records: 'For though the fig-tree shall not blossom, Neither shall the fruit be in the vines; the labour of the olive shall fail, And the fields shall yield no meat; The flock shall be cut off from the fold, and there shall be no herd in the stalls: Yet I will rejoice in the Lord, I will joy in the God of my salvation.' But Habakkuk's *Te Deum* was possible only because he worshipped the God of his salvation. His God was more than the God of nature; He was pre-eminently the God of Grace.

If we knew God only as Creator, we might find Him ruthless rather than beneficent. Beneath the calm opulence of nature in summer mood, there is a hidden struggle for existence, for she is still 'Nature, red in tooth and claw'. The distinguished American humanist, Paul Elmer More, found it possible to visit one of England's loveliest beauty-spots and yet to sense a divine indifference to life. As he stood on Symond's Yat, he thought of the gigantic destructive forces of Nature that had built up the valley beneath him; he imagined the convulsions of molten lava that cooled to form the mountains, and the vast swirling of waters that centuries before scooped out the river-basin. Then he turned to contemplate the apparently calm scene below: the birds sailing like confident ships on the seas of mild air and the gentle, stolid ox grazing so placidly and contentedly on the riverside meadow. 'To the eye it was a wide-spread theatre of joy,' wrote More, 'and a masque of peaceful beauty. Until I thought of what lay beneath the surface. Here, in fact, was an army of countless individuals, each driven on by an instinctive lust of life as if engaged on a vast internecine warfare—each blade of grass fighting for its place under the sun and obtaining it by the suppression of some other plant, each animal preying for sustenance upon some other form of life. It is a system of ruthless competition and remorseless extermination.' His final verdict on the scene was: 'From every spot of the earth rises continually the battle-cry of Nature: *Vae victis*.'[3]

We can worship God when we see the golden corn dancing in the summer sunlight; but can we worship Him when we see a snake gliding through the grass towards a hypnotized bird? We can praise Him for the lark's glad carol; can we praise Him for the bloodthirsty baying of the hounds? We can thank Him for the sunshine and the rains that drop out of the heavens; can we thank Him for the hawk that drops on the field-mouse out of the same sky?

III

It seems that we can be certain of God's over-ruling providence in nature only after we have known His benevolence in grace. We can thank Him for our creation, only after we have experienced His re-creation in Christ.

In nature He may seem capricious, like nature's own changing moods; in Christ He is known as eternal and unchanging Holy Love. In nature He is seen as absolute Power and infinite Wisdom; in Jesus Christ alone is He revealed as invincible Love. In nature God seems to be remote and austere, if not inimical, dwelling amid an arsenal of thunderbolts, earthquakes and deluges; in Christ alone He is 'Emmanuel', God-with-us.

The peril of nature-worship is that it is a substitute for the worship of God who is Creator, Redeemer and Sanctifier. Grateful as Christians must be for the gifts of nature, their chief cause for thanksgiving to God is 'His unspeakable gift'. In the majestic and comprehensive words of the *General*

---

[3] *The Sceptical Approach to Religion* (Princeton University Press), pp. 78-80, cited by H. H. Farmer, *The World and God* (Nisbet, 1935), pp. 279-80.

Thanksgiving: 'We bless Thee for our creation, preservation, and all the blessings of this life; but, *above all,* for Thine inestimable love in the redemption of the world by our Lord Jesus Christ; for the means of grace and for the hope of glory.'

In Christ we are no longer orphans of the universe. The God of nature is seen to be our Father, and Christ becomes our Elder Brother. We know that the world's greatest privilege is to belong to the Christian family which gathers in His House, the Church, offering Him the sacrifice of praise.

Our aim will be that of Coleridge's *Ancient Mariner*, who knew the desolation and ruthlessness of nature:

> 'To walk together to the kirk
> With a goodly company.
> . . . .
> To walk together to the kirk
> And all together pray,
> While each to his great Father bends,
> Old men and babes, and loving friends,
> And youth and maidens gay.'

The Christian Family fittingly adores God in God's House, as God's Household.

IV

It remains only to answer those who aver that formal worship in a church is a departure from the simplicity and spontaneity of the house-fellowship of the Church of the Apostles. This criticism was finely repelled by Richard Hooker, the distinguished Elizabethan Anglican apologist, in the following words:

'The Church of Christ which was in Jerusalem, and held that profession which had not the public allowance and countenance of authority, could not so long use the exercise of Christian religion, but in private only. So that as Jews they had access to the Temple and synagogues, where God was served after the custom of the Law; but that for which they did as Christians, they were of necessity forced otherwise to assemble themselves.'[4]

The Christians of primitive days met in houses for their distinctively Christian exercises, because they could not celebrate the Lord's Supper in temple or synagogue. What was an irksome necessity for them, ought not to be elevated into an example for future generations freed from their restrictions.

While it is true that worship is acceptable to God wherever it is offered, so long as it be 'in spirit and in truth', yet

'the very majesty and holiness of the place where God is worshipped, hath *in regard of us* great virtue, force, and efficacy, for that it serveth as a sensible help to stir up devotion, and in that respect no doubt bettereth even our holiest and best actions in this kind.'[5]

Thus the building in which the congregation of Christ meets for worship is more than a convenient roof and walls; it is a 'help to stir up devotion'.

Ancient cathedrals or historic meeting-houses remind the worshippers that 'other men have laboured and ye have entered into their labours'; that the Christian Church has weathered many storms and that 'the gates of hell shall not prevail against it'. Futhermore, they serve as a perpetual reminder of the communion of saints.

The chief advantage of a Christian edifice of worship is that it preaches to the eye, as sermons preach to the ear. The central cross on rood-screen or on communion-table, declares the costliness of our redemption. The stained-glass windows portray, it may be, the prophets, apostles and martyrs, and remind the worshippers of 'the great cloud of witnesses'.

[4] *Of the Laws of Ecclesiastical Polity*, Bk. V, section XI, 2.
[5] *op. cit.*, Bk. V, section XVI, 2.

Or, they may illustrate some incident in the life of our Lord, His holy nativity, His temptations in the wilderness, His miracles, His crucifixion, His resurrection, or the final Judgment at which He is to be the arbiter of human destiny. This is visual teaching of the faith, the use of 'eye-gate' as an avenue to the soul.

The font itself is a reminder that the promises of the Gospel belong as of right to the children of Christian parents. The altar or communion-table betokens the centrality of the sacrament of Holy Communion, and the pulpit or lectern, on which rests the Bible, is an effective reminder to 'search the Scriptures'.

The very beauty of the building is an incentive to 'worship the Lord in the beauty of holiness'. Even a Puritan poet, Milton, could write:

> 'But let my due feet never fail
> To walk the studious cloisters pale,
> And love the high-embower'd roof,
> With antic pillars massy proof,
> And storied windows, richly dight,
> Casting a dim religious light.'[6]

In conclusion, Christian communities have ordinarily worshipped in cathedrals, churches, chapels or meeting-houses, because corporate worship demanded a convenient edifice. In the second place, they have found that the associations and the symbols have assisted the worshippers in their devotions. No sensitive person can answer Hooker's question, except in the negative, when he asks:

> 'Can we judge it a thing seemly for any man to go about the building of a house to the God of heaven with no other appearance, than if his end were to rear up a kitchen or a parlour for his own use?'[7]

[6] Il Penseroso, lines 155-160.
[7] Hooker op. cit., Bk. V, section xii, 1.

A SHORT BIBLIOGRAPHY

G. G. Atkins: *Modern Religious Cults and Movements*

James Black: *New Forms of the Old Faith*

Elmer T. Clark: *The Small Sects in America*

H. H. Farmer: *Towards Belief in God*

H. A. L. Fisher: *Our New Religion*

Bede Frost: *Some Modern Substitutes for Christianity*

William James: *The Varieties of Religious Experience*

H. Richard Niebuhr: *The Social Sources of Denominationalism*

R. Pike: *Jehovah's Witnesses*

J. B. Pratt: *The Religious Consciousness*

L. B. Radford: *Ancient Heresies in Modern Dress*

Clement F. Rogers: *Astrology and Prediction*

J. K. van Baalen: *The Chaos of Cults*

G. Williamson: *Inside Buchmanism*

ACKNOWLEDGMENT

Two quotations (pp. 21 and 105) are used by the courtesy of Hodder and Stoughton Ltd., from the Moffatt Translation of the Bible

INDEX